The Elite Gourmet Bread Machine Cookbook

A Magic Bread Machine to Make Fragrant, Tasty and Fresh Bread Recipes for Any Occasion, Breakfast, Dessert, Birthday Party, Christmas Party

Hutton Karvennet

Content

Introduction

The Basics of Elite Gourmet Bread Machine

When I was a very small girl, I saw my mom bake fresh bread for the family every now and then. The same love for bread making slowly transferred to me, and now I make sure to treat my kids with tasty bread just how my mom did.

Initially, I used to bake the bread in an oven, but it didn't really turn out the way I wanted it to. So, I thought about switching to a bread maker. That's when my husband gifted me the Elite Gourmet Bread Machine on our wedding anniversary. I couldn't be happier!

This appliance is compact, lightweight, and exceptionally useful when it comes to making different types of bread. It completely changed my bread making experience since it comes with some of the most amazing functions. I love experimenting in the kitchen, and trust me, this appliance is perfect for anyone who is a passionate bread maker! Well, saying that this appliance has made my life a lot easier would surely be an understatement.

Therefore, keeping that in mind, I thought of sharing my experience with you all. The Elite Gourmet Bread Machine Cookbook is filled with 200 recipes that are super easy to make. Apart from that, you will also find all the necessary information when it comes to its specifications, functions, and features.

On top of that, I have also written about some of the accessories that I got along with this appliance. So, without wasting any more time, give this cookbook a read!

Key Specifications

The Elite Gourmet Bread Machine is designed from non-toxic and durable material. Due to its ease of handling, this bread maker can be used by a beginner as well. In this section, I shall discuss some of the key specifications of Elite Gourmet's bread machine.

LCD Display

With the help of the LCD display, everything is clearly indicated. You can select the desired function and press start. The rest will easily be taken care of by the Elite Gourmet Bread Machine in just a few minutes!

Removable and Non-stick Bread Pan

The bread pan of Elite Gourmet Bread Machine can be removed from the appliance. In addition to that, it also features a non-stick coating, which makes it easy to clean. When you remove the pan from the machine, it gives you the freedom to clean the interior without making a lot of mess.

Removable Kneading Paddle

After removing the bread from the pan, you might notice that there are ugly marks from the kneading paddle. While this small part inside the pan can help you form a consistent batter, it can also be a source of annoyance. So, when it comes to baking your favorite bread in Elite Gourmet, you can keep this worry aside! It allows you to remove the kneading paddle once its job is done, and can enjoy a spot-free bread.

Convection Cooking

With the help of the convection cooking, the heat inside the appliance gets circulated evenly. The Elite Gourmet Bread Machine also works along the same lines and makes sure that nothing remains uncooked. On top of that, it also helps to cook the food quickly.

Main Functions

Baking loaves of bread with Elite Gourmet Bread Machine is super-easy and ensures that you never get tired of experimenting. You only have to follow these steps mentioned below:

▸ Add ingredients

▸ Select the cycle

▸ Press start

See easy-peasy! This programmable machine gives you the option to choose from three loaf sizes and nineteen baking functions. Take a look!

Basic

Here is the easiest way to bake bread that everyone loves! With the basic function, you can easily bake the standard white bread and relish it with jam or butter.

Quick

The quick menu will help you bake your bread a lot faster than the normal time. It is because this function doesn't require the use of yeast. Therefore, if you don't want to wait for a long period to make healthy bread for your family, this is the correct option!

Sweet

The sweet setting on Elite Gourmet Bread Machine will help you bake soft and fluffy bread. It is usually filled with jam or cream cheese, which makes it ideal for a dessert idea. Well, this particular function is my favorite!

Whole wheat

To make one of the healthiest bread recipes, you don't have to look for a separate appliance. The bread maker from Elite Gourmet has an option to bake whole wheat bread. Just add special bread flour and a little bit of honey.

French

French bread is longer and narrower than regular bread. In addition to that, it is also hard and crusty on the outside and has a soft and light crumb. Want to try your hands on this recipe? Well, the Elite Gourmet Bread Maker is at your disposal! By selecting its French function, you can bake a crusty loaf of bread just like the original recipe!

Rye

The rye bread is darker and denser as compared to the basic and whole wheat bread. In addition to that, it features less gluten than regular flour bread. Therefore, for an earthy taste, you can choose the rye function.

Gluten-Free

The people who are gluten and dairy intolerant can make gluten-free bread by pressing on this function. Not only is it super healthy, but it also tastes better than regular gluten-free bread.

Rice Bread

While making this type of bread, you use rice flour instead of wheat flour. Rice bread is an exceptional substitute for gluten-free bread and will not cause reactions to people who are gluten-intolerant.

Sandwich

Sandwich bread is prepared specifically for sandwiches. Therefore, if your kids are in the mood to eat a yummy treat, you know what to do!

Cake

With the help of this function, you can mix the cake batter without tiring your arms. Just pour all the ingredients and press the cake function, and your batter will be ready within minutes!

Wholemeal Dough

The wholemeal dough is made using the wheat kernel. It helps in adding flavor and nutrition to baked products, specifically bread.

Pizza Dough

Pizza dough can be made from scratch using the Elite Gourmet Bread Machine. Add flour, yeast, water, olive oil, and put them in the bread pan. Select the Pizza Dough function and make a yummy treat within a few minutes.

Leaven Dough

Leaven dough is used for baking leavened bread. It contains baking yeast, baking soda/powder. These ingredients cause the dough to rise and create a light product. The Leaven Dough function gives you the perfect dough to make light and airy bread.

Knead

Kneading is the process of making dough for bread. It requires a person to mix the ingredients, such as flour and water, to strengthen the final product using their hands. Therefore, to save you from putting a lot of effort, simply put these ingredients into the bread pan and select the desired function.

Mix

The mix function in Elite Gourmet Bread Machine helps you mix the ingredients of any type of bread with consistency.

Jam

Want to make jam at home? Well, you got this! The Elite Gourmet Bread Machine comes with an in-built jam-making function, which will help you enjoy homemade jam with ease. From strawberries to apples, you can put any type of fruit inside the bread pan and add granulated sugar, lemon juice, and pectin. Select the jam function and wait for the timer to stop. Pour the mixture into a jar and keep it in the fridge after it gets cool.

Yogurt

Yogurt is one of my favorite dairy products that fill my tummy in just a couple of spoons. Usually, I prefer making yogurt at home, and this wonderful kitchen appliance has made it all the more convenient for me!

The process is simple. Add the required amount of milk to the pan, and then pour in some yogurt. Close the lid and press the yogurt option. In the next few hours, you can savor the yummy homemade yogurt!

Defrost

This option makes sure that you do not waste the leftover bread that sits on the corner of your refrigerator. Take out as many slices from the fridge and place them inside the pan. Now select the defrost option from the menu. The slices of the bread will taste fresh, and you won't even have to waste any food.

Essential Features

Now that I have explained the key specifications and the different functions of the Elite Gourmet Bread Machine, it's time we move to another section. Here, I will talk about all the essential features of this lightweight and super-functional bread maker. So, without further ado, let's just dive straight into the features.

Delay Start Function

Most of the time, bread machines come with a delayed start timer. This function allows you to add all the bread ingredients and set a timer. After the timer is over, the machine switches on its own. Usually, it is done overnight so that you can enjoy fresh bread right when you wake up. Not only that, but you can set it in the morning and come home to freshly baked bread.

The Elite Gourmet Bread Machine comes with a 15-hour delay time. This way, you get freshly baked bread the moment you want to eat it.

Indicator Light

This bread maker by Elite Gourmet comes with indicator light. It tells you exactly when your food is ready.

Viewing Window

The viewing window on Elite Gourmet Bread Machine lets you see if your food is getting cooked properly or not. It is on top of the lid.

Cool-Touch Exterior

The exterior of this appliance remains cool even after cooking your favorite type of bread. This ensures that you do not burn your hand while taking the bread out of the appliance.

Keep Warm Setting

Even after the food is cooked, you can keep it inside the bread maker. The Keep Warm Setting makes sure that the food remains warm for around 60 minutes.

Anti-slip Silicone Feet

The bread-making machine features anti-slip silicone feet, which prevents it from falling from the counter.

Package Included

Apart from the Elite Gourmet Bread Machine, you will find several accessories in the package. These will help you make the baking process a lot easier. Take a look at all the things that come with this wonderful cooking appliance.

Measuring cup

A measuring cup will make sure that you do not mess up the measurements of the ingredients that go in a certain food. There are tiny markings on the outer surface of the cup, with the help of which you can figure out the exact amount of stuff that goes in the bread pan.

Bread pan

The bread pan of Elite Gourmet Bread Machine is made from non-stick material, which makes it easy to clean. Apart from that, it also can be removed from the machine with ease, which helps in the holistic cleaning.

Measuring spoon

A measuring spoon helps you to measure the amount of an ingredient. The ingredient can either be liquid, or it can be dry. With the Elite Gourmet Bread Machine, you get a measuring spoon that can be used to put every ingredient in the perfect quantity.

Metal hook to lift the kneading paddle

This accessory is used to lift the kneading paddle from the bread pan with ease. Therefore, you won't have to put in a lot of effort while removing it from the pan.

Kneading blade

The kneading blade helps mix all the ingredients to form a solid batter, which can be later used to bake different types of bread. The best part about this blade is that it can be removed from the bread pan. It makes sure that your bread comes out all nice and clean without any deformity.

Basic Breads

Chapter 1

Sourdough Bread

Serves 12

Sourdough Starter:

- 1½ teaspoons quick active dry yeast
- 4 cups warm water

- 3 cups all-purpose flour
- 4 teaspoons sugar

Bread:

- ½ cup water
- 3 cups bread flour
- 2 tablespoons sugar

- 1½ teaspoons salt
- 1 teaspoon quick active dry yeast

1. Prepare the sourdough starter at least one week before baking the bread by dissolving 1½ teaspoons yeast in warm water in a glass bowl.
2. Stir in 3 cups flour and the 4 teaspoons sugar. Beat with electric mixer on medium speed for 1 minute or until smooth.
3. Cover loosely and let stand at room temperature for one week or until mixture is bubbly and has a sour aroma; when ready, cover tight and refrigerate until ready to use.
4. When you are ready to bake the bread, measure out 1 cup of the sourdough starter and all of the remaining bread ingredients carefully, placing in bread machine pan the wet ingredients first, then dry ingredients.
5. Select Basic and Medium Crust, then press Start.
6. Remove baked bread from pan and cool on a wire rack.

White Bread

Serves 16

- 1 cup warm water
- 2 tablespoons agave nectar
- ¼ cup applesauce

- 3 cups bread flour
- 1 teaspoon salt
- 2¼ teaspoons rapid rise yeast

1. Add liquid ingredients to the bread pan.
2. Measure and add dry ingredients (except yeast) to the bread pan.
3. Make a well in the center of the dry ingredients and add the yeast.
4. Snap the baking pan into the bread machine and close the lid.
5. Choose the Basic cycle, preferred crust color and press Start.
6. Remove and allow to cool on a wire rack when baked, before serving.

Honey Bread

Serves 12

- 4½ cups 100% whole wheat flour
- 1½ cups warm water
- ⅓ cup olive oil
- ⅓ cup honey
- 2 teaspoons salt
- 1 tablespoon active dry yeast

1. Add water to the bread machine.
2. Measure and add the oil first, then the honey in the same measuring cup: this will make the honey slip out of the measuring cup more easily.
3. Add salt, then flour.
4. Make a small well in the flour and add the yeast.
5. Set to Wheat Bread cycle, choose crust color, and press Start.
6. Remove and allow to cool on a wire rack when baked, before serving.

Buttery Dinner Rolls

Serves 16

- ½ cup warm water
- ½ cup warm milk
- 1 egg
- ⅓ cup butter, unsalted and softened
- ⅓ cup sugar
- 1 teaspoon salt
- 3¾ cups all-purpose flour
- 1 (¼-ounce / 7.1-g) package active dry yeast
- ¼ cup butter, softened
- Flour, for surface

1. Place ingredients in the bread pan in the following order: water, milk, egg, butter, sugar, salt, and flour. Reserve yeast.
2. Make a well in the center of the dry ingredients and add the yeast.
3. Select Dough cycle and press Start.
4. When cycle finishes, turn dough out onto a lightly floured surface.
5. Divide dough in half and roll each half into a 12-inch circle, spread ¼ cup softened butter over entire round. Cut each circle into 8 wedges. Roll wedges starting at the wide end and roll gently but tight.
6. Place point side down on ungreased cookie sheet. Cover with clean kitchen towel and put in a warm place, let rise 1 hour.
7. Preheat oven to 400ºF (205ºC) and bake rolls in preheated oven for 10 to 15 minutes, until golden.
8. Serve warm.

Caraway Rye Bread

Serves 12

- 1 cup water
- 1½ teaspoons salt
- 2 tablespoons sugar
- 1 tablespoon butter
- 2 teaspoons caraway seed
- 2 cups bread flour
- 1 cup rye flour
- 1½ teaspoons quick active yeast

1. Place all of the ingredients except yeast in the bread machine pan in the order listed.
2. Make a well in the center of the dry ingredients and add the yeast.
3. Choose the Basic cycle for 1½-pound (680-g) loaf and medium crust color. Press Start.
4. Remove bread when done and allow to cool for 10 minutes before slicing with a bread knife.

Easy Cracked Wheat Bread

Serves 10

- 1¼ cup plus 1 tablespoon water
- 2 tablespoons vegetable oil
- 3 cups bread flour
- ¾ cup cracked wheat
- 1½ teaspoons salt
- 2 tablespoons sugar
- 2¼ teaspoons active dry yeast

1. Bring water to a boil.
2. Place cracked wheat in small mixing bowl, pour water over it and stir.
3. Cool to 80ºF (27ºC).
4. Place cracked wheat mixture into pan, followed by all ingredients (except yeast) in the order listed.
5. Make a well in the center of the dry ingredients and add the yeast.
6. Select the Basic cycle, medium color crust, and press Start.
7. Check dough consistency after 5 minutes of kneading. The dough should be a soft, tacky ball. If it is dry and stiff, add water one ½ tablespoon at a time until sticky. If it's too wet and sticky, add 1 tablespoon of flour at a time.
8. Remove bread when cycle is finished and allow to cool before serving.

Mashed Potato Bread

Serves 12

- ¾ cup water
- ⅔ cup instant mashed potatoes
- 1 egg
- 2 tablespoons butter, unsalted
- 2 tablespoons white sugar
- ¼ cup dry milk powder
- 1 teaspoon salt
- 3 cups bread flour
- 1½ teaspoons active dry yeast

1. Add the ingredients to bread machine in the order listed above. Reserve yeast for next step.
2. Make a well in the center of the dry ingredients and add the yeast.
3. Press the Basic cycle, choose light to medium crust color, and press Start.
4. Remove from bread pan and allow to cool on a wire rack before serving.

Basic Pumpernickel Bread

Serves 12

- 1¼ cups lukewarm water
- ¼ cup molasses
- 2 tablespoons unsweetened cocoa powder
- 1 teaspoon sea salt
- 1 cup whole wheat flour
- 1 cup rye flour
- 2 cups unbleached all-purpose flour
- 2½ tablespoons vegetable oil
- 1½ tablespoons packed brown sugar
- 1 tablespoon caraway seeds
- 2½ teaspoons instant yeast

1. Note: all ingredients should be at room temperature before baking.
2. Add all of the ingredients in the order listed above, reserving yeast.
3. Make a well in the center of the dry ingredients and add the yeast .
4. Set the bread machine on Whole Wheat cycle, select crust color, and press Start.
5. Remove and let the loaf cool for 15 minutes before slicing.

Hearty Multigrain Bread

Serves 12

- 2¼ cups whole wheat flour
- ¾ cup ground oatmeal
- 2 tablespoons wheat bran
- 2 tablespoons flaxseed meal
- 2 tablespoons vital wheat gluten
- 1 tablespoon dough enhancer
- 1 teaspoon salt
- 2⅔ teaspoons active dry yeast
- 2 tablespoons olive oil
- 1 tablespoon agave nectar
- 1 tablespoon brown sugar
- 1 cup warm water (slightly warmer than room temperature)

1. Set the yeast aside and combine the remaining dry ingredients in a mixing bowl.
2. Add the liquids to the bread machine first, followed by the dry ingredients.
3. Make a small well in the flour and add the yeast.
4. Press Whole Wheat cycle, light crust color, and press Start.
5. Remove loaf when done and lay on a cooling rack until cool to slice.

Poppy Seed White Bread

Serves 12

- 2 tablespoons full rounded yeast
- 2 cups white bread flour
- 1½ tablespoons sugar
- 1 tablespoon salt
- 1 cup water

For the Topping:

- Olive oil
- Poppy seeds

1. Add water first, then add the dry ingredients to the bread machine, reserving yeast.
2. Make a well in the center of the dry ingredients and add the yeast.
3. Choose French cycle, light crust color, and push Start.
4. When bread is finished, coat the top of loaf with a little olive oil and lightly sprinkle with poppy seeds.
5. Allow to cool slightly and serve warm with extra olive oil for dipping.

Cinnamon Friendship Bread

Serves 12

- 1 cup Amish Friendship Bread Starter
- 3 eggs
- ⅔ cup vegetable oil
- ¼ cup milk
- 1 cup sugar
- ½ teaspoon vanilla extract
- 2 teaspoons cinnamon
- 1½ teaspoons baking powder
- ½ teaspoon salt
- ½ teaspoon baking soda
- 2 cups flour
- 2 small boxes instant vanilla pudding

1. Add all of the wet ingredients into the bread machine pan.
2. Add in dry ingredients, except sugar and cinnamon.
3. Set bread machine on Sweet cycle, light crust color and press Start.
4. During the last 30 minutes of baking, lift lid and quickly add ¼ cup sugar and ¼ teaspoon of cinnamon.
5. When finished baking, leave in bread machine for 20 minutes to rest.
6. Remove from baking pan and put loaf on a cooling rack.

Basic Slider Buns

Serves 18

- 1¼ cups milk
- 1 egg
- 2 tablespoons butter
- ¾ teaspoon salt
- ¼ cup white sugar
- 3¾ cups all-purpose flour
- 1 package active dry yeast
- Flour, for surface

1. Add all ingredients to the pan of your bread machine in the order listed above.
2. Set bread machine to Dough cycle. Once the Dough cycle is complete, roll dough out on a floured surface to about a 1-inch thickness.
3. Cut out 18 buns with a biscuit cutter or small glass and place them on a greased baking sheet.
4. Let buns rise about one hour or until they have doubled in size.
5. Bake at 350ºF (180ºC) for 10 minutes.
6. Brush the tops of baked buns with melted butter and serve.

Vanilla Brioche

Serves 12

- ¼ cup milk
- 2 eggs
- 4 tablespoons butter
- 1½ tablespoons vanilla sugar
- ¼ teaspoon salt
- 2 cups flour
- 1½ teaspoon yeast
- 1 egg white, for finishing

1. Place wet ingredients (except egg white for finishing) into your bread machine.
2. Add dry ingredients, except for yeast.
3. Make a well inside the flour and then add the yeast into the well.
4. Set to Dough cycle and press Start.
5. Remove dough, place dough on floured surface and divide into 12 equal size rolls.
6. Pinch walnut-sized ball of dough off each roll, making a smaller ball; make indent on top of roll and wet with milk; attach small ball to top making the traditional brioche shape.
7. Let rise for 30 minutes until almost double in size.
8. Preheat oven to 375ºF (190ºC).
9. Beat egg white, brush tops of brioche rolls, and bake at 375ºF (190ºC) for 10 to 12 minutes, or until golden on top. Cool on rack before serving.

Almond Bread

Serves 12

- 1 cup, plus 2 tablespoons water
- 3 tablespoons agave nectar
- 2 tablespoons butter, unsalted
- 1½ cups bread flour
- 1½ cups whole wheat flour
- ¼ cup slivered almonds, toasted
- 1 teaspoon salt
- 1½ teaspoons quick active dry yeast

1. Add all of the ingredients in bread machine pan in the order they appear above, reserving yeast.
2. Make a well in the center of the dry ingredients and add the yeast.
3. Select the Basic cycle, light or medium crust color, and press Start.
4. Remove baked bread from pan and cool on a rack before slicing.

Hamburger and Hot Dog Buns

Serves 8 to 10

- 1¼ cups milk, slightly warmed
- 1 egg, beaten
- 2 tablespoons butter, unsalted
- ¼ cup white sugar
- ¾ teaspoon salt
- 3¾ cups bread flour
- 1¼ teaspoons active dry yeast
- Flour, for surface

1. Place all ingredients into the pan of the bread machine in the following order, reserving yeast: milk, egg, butter, sugar, salt, flour.
2. Make a well in the center of the dry ingredients and add the yeast.
3. Select Dough cycle. When cycle is complete, turn out onto floured surface.
4. Cut dough in half and roll each half out to a 1" thick circle.
5. Cut each half into 6 (3½") rounds with inverted glass as a cutter. (For hot dog buns, cut lengthwise into 1-inch-thick rolls, and cut a slit along the length of the bun for easier separation later.)
6. Place on a greased baking sheet far apart and brush with melted butter.
7. Cover and let rise until doubled, about one hour; preheat an oven to 350ºF (180ºC).
8. Bake for 9 minutes.
9. Let cool and serve with your favorite meats and toppings!

Cornbread

Serves 10

- 2 fresh eggs, at room temperature
- 1 cup milk
- ¼ cup butter, unsalted, at room temperature
- ¾ cup sugar
- 1 teaspoon salt
- 2 cups unbleached all-purpose flour
- 1 cup cornmeal
- 1 tablespoon baking powder

1. Add all of the ingredients to your bread machine in the order listed.
2. Select the Quick Bread cycle, light crust color, and press Start.
3. Allow to cool for five minutes on a wire rack and serve warm.

Basic Pretzel Rolls

Serves 4

- 1 cup warm water
- 1 egg white, beaten
- 2 tablespoons oil
- 3 cups all-purpose flour
- ½ teaspoon salt
- 1 tablespoon granulated sugar
- 1 package dry yeast
- Coarse sea salt, for topping
- $\frac{1}{3}$ cup baking soda (for boiling process)
- Flour, for surface

1. Place the ingredients in bread machine pan in the order listed above, reserving yeast
2. Make a well in the center of the dry ingredients and add the yeast.
3. Select Dough cycle and press Start.
4. Remove the dough out onto a lightly floured surface and divide dough into four parts.
5. Roll the four parts into balls.
6. Place on greased cookie sheet and let rise uncovered for about 20 minutes or until puffy.
7. In a 3-quart saucepan, combine 2 quarts of water and baking soda and bring to a boil.
8. Preheat an oven to 425ºF (220ºC).
9. Lower 2 pretzels into the saucepan and simmer for 10 seconds on each side.
10. Lift from water with a slotted spoon and return to greased cookie sheet; repeat with remaining pretzels.
11. Let dry briefly.
12. Brush with egg white and sprinkle with coarse salt.
13. Bake in preheated oven for 20 minutes or until golden brown.
14. Let cool slightly before serving.

Italian Breadsticks

Serves 12 to 16

- 1½ cups warm water
- 2 tablespoons butter, unsalted and melted
- 4¼ cups bread flour
- 2 tablespoons sugar
- 1 tablespoon salt
- 1 package active dry yeast

For the Topping:

- 1 stick unsalted butter, melted
- 2 teaspoons garlic powder
- 1 teaspoons salt
- 1 teaspoon parsley

1. Add wet ingredients to your bread machine pan.
2. Mix dry ingredients, except yeast, and add to pan.
3. Make a well in the center of the dry ingredients and add the yeast.
4. Set to Dough cycle and press Start.
5. When the dough is done, roll out and cut into strips; keep in mind that they will double in size after they have risen, so roll them out thinner than a typical breadstick to yield room for them to grow.
6. Place on a greased baking sheet.
7. Cover the dough with a light towel and let sit in a warm area for 45 minutes to an hour.
8. Preheat an oven to 400ºF (205ºC).
9. Bake breadsticks for 6 to 7 minutes.
10. Mix the melted butter, garlic powder, salt and parsley in a small mixing bowl.
11. Brush the bread sticks with half the butter mixture; return to oven and bake for 5 to 8 additional minutes.
12. Remove breadsticks from the oven and brush the other half of the butter mixture.
13. Allow to cool for a few minutes before serving.

Corn Bagels

Serves 9

- 1 cup warm water
- 1½ teaspoons salt
- 2 tablespoons sugar
- 3 cups bread flour
- 2¼ teaspoons active dry yeast
- 3 quarts boiling water
- 3 tablespoons white sugar
- 1 tablespoon cornmeal
- 1 egg white
- Flour, for surface

1. Place in the bread machine pan in the following order: warm water, salt, sugar, and flour.
2. Make a well in the center of the dry ingredients and add the yeast.
3. Select Dough cycle and press Start.
4. When Dough cycle is complete, remove pan and let dough rest on a lightly floured surface. Stir 3 tablespoons of sugar into the boiling water.
5. Cut dough into 9 equal pieces and roll each piece into a small ball.
6. Flatten each ball with the palm of your hand. Poke a hole in the middle of each using your thumb. Twirl the dough on your finger to make the hole bigger, while evening out the dough around the hole.
7. Sprinkle an ungreased baking sheet with 1 teaspoon cornmeal. Place the bagel on the baking sheet and repeat until all bagels are formed.
8. Cover the shaped bagels with a clean kitchen towel and let rise for 10 minutes.
9. Preheat an oven to 375ºF (190ºC).
10. Carefully transfer the bagels, one by one, to the boiling water. Boil for 1 minute, turning halfway.
11. Drain on a clean towel. Arrange boiled bagels on the baking sheet.
12. Glaze the tops with egg white and sprinkle any toppings you desire.
13. Bake for 20 to 25 minutes or until golden brown.
14. Let cool on a wire rack before serving.

Breakfast Breads

Chapter 2

Breakfast Cinnamon Swirl

Makes 2 pounds

For the Dough:

- 1⅓ cups water
- 3 tablespoons unsalted butter, cut into pieces
- ⅓ cup sugar
- 4 cups bread flour
- ¼ cup dry buttermilk powder

- 1 tablespoon plus 1 teaspoon gluten
- 1½ teaspoons salt
- 2½ teaspoons SAF yeast or 1 tablespoon bread machine yeast

For the Cinnamon Swirl:

- 2 tablespoons unsalted butter, melted, for brushing

- ⅓ cup light brown sugar
- 1 tablespoon ground cinnamon

1. Place all the ingredients in the pan according to the order in the manufacturer's instructions. Set crust on medium and set to Basic cycle.

2. After Rise 2 ends on the Basic cycle, press Pause, remove the pan, and close the lid. Immediately turn the dough out onto a lightly floured work surface; pat into an 8-by-12-inch fat rectangle. Brush with the melted butter. Sprinkle with the sugar and cinnamon, leaving a 1-inch space all the way around the edge. Starting at a short edge, roll the dough up jelly-roll fashion. Tuck the ends under and pinch the bottom seam. Coat the bottom of the dough with cooking spray, remove the kneading blade, and place the dough back in the pan; press Start to continue to rise and bake as programmed. When the baking cycle ends, immediately remove the bread from the pan.

3. When the machine beeps at the end of the cycle, remove the pan and turn the dough out onto a lightly floured work surface. Pat the the 2 pounds (907 g) dough into two 8-by-12-inch rectangles. Brush the rectangle(s) with melted butter. Sprinkle with the brown sugar and cinnamon, leaving a 1-inch edge all the way around. Starting at a short end, roll up jelly-roll fashion. Tuck the ends under and pinch the bottom seam.

4. Place the single large loaf in the prepared 9-by-5-inch pan or the two smaller loaves in the 7-by-4-inch pans. Spray the top(s) with cooking spray and cover lightly with plastic wrap. Let rise at room temperature until doubled in bulk, about 45 minutes. Bake for 35 to 40 minutes, or until golden brown and the sides have slightly contracted from the pan. If the crust browns too quickly, place a piece of aluminum foil loosely over the top.

5. Place the bread on a rack and let cool to room temperature before slicing. Dust with plain or vanilla confectioners' sugar, if desired.

Pecan and Apple Bread

Makes 2 pounds

- 1½ cups buttermilk
- 2½ tablespoons walnut oil
- 4 cups bread flour
- ¼ cup light brown sugar
- 1 tablespoon plus 1 teaspoon gluten
- 1½ teaspoons salt
- 1⅓ tablespoons ground cinnamon
- 2½ teaspoons SAF yeast or 1 tablespoon bread machine yeast
- ⅔ cup chopped dried apples
- ½ cup chopped pecans

1. Place the ingredients, except the apples and pecans, in the pan according to the order in the manufacturer's instructions. Set crust on medium and program for the Basic or Fruit and Nut cycle; press Start. When the machine beeps, or between Knead 1 and Knead 2, add the apples and pecans.
2. When the baking cycle ends, immediately remove the bread from the pan and place it on a rack. Let cool to room temperature before slicing.

Raisin Bread

Makes 2 pounds

- 1⅓ cups dark raisins
- 1½ cups buttermilk
- 1 large egg
- 2½ tablespoons canola oil
- 3 tablespoons dark brown sugar
- 4 cups bread flour
- 1 tablespoon plus 2 teaspoons gluten
- 2 teaspoons salt
- 2¼ teaspoons SAF yeast or 2¾ teaspoons bread machine yeast

1. Place the raisins in a small bowl to heat in the microwave or in a small pan to heat on the stove. Cover with water and heat to boiling. Let stand for 10 minutes to plump, then drain on paper towels.
2. Place the ingredients, except the raisins, in the pan according to the order in the manufacturer's instructions. Set crust on medium and program for the Sweet Bread or Fruit and Nut cycle; press Start. When the machine beeps, or between Knead 1 and Knead 2, add the raisins.
3. When the baking cycle ends, immediately remove the bread from the pan and place it on a rack. Let cool to room temperature before slicing.

Poppy Seed Prune Bread

Makes 2 pounds

- ²/₃ cup milk
- ½ cup water
- 3 tablespoons unsalted butter, cut into pieces
- 1 large egg
- 3 cups bread flour
- 1 cup whole wheat pastry flour
- ¼ cup plus 1 tablespoon poppy seeds
- 3 tablespoons sugar
- Grated zest of 1 lemon
- 1 tablespoon plus 1 teaspoon gluten
- 2 teaspoons salt
- 2½ teaspoons SAF yeast or 1 tablespoon bread machine yeast
- ¾ cup chopped pitted prunes

1. Place the ingredients, except the prunes, in the pan according to the order in the manufacturer's instructions. Set crust on medium and program for the Basic or Fruit and Nut cycle; press Start. When the machine beeps, or between Knead 1 and Knead 2, add the prunes.
2. When the baking cycle ends, immediately remove the bread from the pan and place it on a rack. Let cool to room temperature before slicing.

Golden Raisin and Cranberry Bread

Makes 2 pounds

- 1²/₃ cups water
- 2½ tablespoons unsalted butter, melted
- 3 tablespoons light brown sugar
- 4 cups bread flour
- ¹/₃ cup nonfat dry milk
- 1 tablespoon plus 2 teaspoons gluten
- 2 teaspoons salt
- 1¼ teaspoons ground cardamom
- 2½ teaspoons SAF yeast or 1 tablespoon bread machine yeast
- ¾ cup golden raisins
- ¾ cup dried cranberries

1. Place the ingredients, except the fruit, in the pan according to the order in the manufacturer's instructions. Set crust on light and program for the Sweet Bread or Fruit and Nut cycle; press Start. When the machine beeps, or between Knead 1 and Knead 2, add the fruit.
2. When the baking cycle ends, immediately remove the bread from the pan and place it on a rack. Let cool to room temperature before slicing.

Banana and Macadamia Oatmeal Bread

Makes 2 pounds

- 1 1/3 cups milk
- 3 tablespoons unsalted butter, cut into pieces
- 1 (8-ounce / 227-g) banana, sliced
- 2½ cups bread flour
- 1½ cups whole wheat pastry flour
- ¾ cup rolled oats
- 3 tablespoons sugar
- 1 tablespoon plus 1 teaspoon gluten
- 1¼ teaspoons salt
- 1 tablespoon SAF yeast or 1 tablespoon plus ½ teaspoon bread machine yeast
- ½ cup chopped salted macadamia nuts

1. Place the ingredients, except the nuts, in the pan according to the order in the manufacturer's instructions. Set crust on medium and program for the Sweet Bread or Fruit and Nut cycle; press Start. When the machine beeps, or between Knead 1 and Knead 2, add the macadamia nuts.
2. When the baking cycle ends, immediately remove the bread from the pan and place it on a rack. Let cool to room temperature before slicing.

Chocolate, Apricot, and Walnut Orange Bread

Makes 2 pounds

- 1¾ cups mandarin orange segments, liquid reserved
- 3 tablespoons reserved orange liquid or orange liqueur
- 4 tablespoons unsalted butter, cut into pieces
- 4 cups bread flour
- 1/3 cup sugar
- 1 tablespoon gluten
- 2 teaspoons salt
- 2¼ teaspoons SAF yeast or 2¾ teaspoons bread machine yeast
- 2/3 cup white chocolate chips
- ½ cup minced dried apricots
- ½ cup chopped walnuts

1. Place the ingredients, except the white chocolate chips, apricots, and walnuts, in the pan according to the order in the manufacturer's instructions. Set crust on medium and program for the Basic or Sweet Bread cycle; press Start. The dough ball will ini-tially look dry; do not be tempted to add more liquid. When the machine beeps, or between Knead 1 and Knead 2, add the chips, apricots, and walnuts.
2. When the baking cycle ends, immediately remove the bread from the pan and place it on a rack. Let cool to room temperature before slicing.

Pumpkin and Cranberry Bread

Makes 2 pounds

- 1 cup dried cranberries
- 3 tablespoons brandy
- 1 cup water
- ½ cup pumpkin purée
- 3 tablespoons nut oil
- 4 cups bread flour
- ¼ cup light brown sugar
- 3 tablespoons dry buttermilk
- powder
- 1 tablespoon plus 1 teaspoon gluten
- 2 teaspoons salt
- 1¾ teaspoons pumpkin or apple pie spice
- 2½ teaspoons SAF yeast or 1 tablespoon bread machine yeast

1. Sprinkle the dried cranberries with the brandy in a small bowl. Cover with plastic wrap and let stand at room temperature for 1 hour to macerate.
2. Place the ingredients, except the cranberries, in the pan according to the order in the manufacturer's instructions. Set crust on medium and program for the Sweet Bread cycle; press Start. When the machine beeps, or between Knead 1 and Knead 2, add the cranberries and any extra brandy in the bowl.
3. When the baking cycle ends, immediately remove the bread from the pan and place it on a rack. Let cool to room temperature before slicing.

Cinnamon Granola Bread

Makes 2 pounds

- 1½ cups buttermilk
- 3 tablespoons vegetable oil
- 3 tablespoons honey
- 2¾ cups bread flour
- 1 cup whole wheat flour
- 1⅓ cups granola
- 1 tablespoon plus 1 teaspoon gluten
- 2 teaspoons salt
- 1½ teaspoons ground cinnamon
- 2½ teaspoons SAF yeast or 1 tablespoon bread machine yeast

1. Place all the ingredients in the pan according to the order in the manufacturer's instructions. Set crust on medium and program for the Basic cycle; press Start.
2. When the baking cycle ends, immediately remove the bread from the pan and place it on a rack. Let cool to room temperature before slicing.

Almond and Cherry Bread

Makes 2 pounds

- 1²/₃ cups milk
- ¾ teaspoon almond extract
- 1½ tablespoons butter, cut into pieces
- 4 tablespoons almond paste, cut into pieces
- 4 cups bread flour
- ¼ cup sugar
- 1 tablespoon plus 1 teaspoon gluten
- 2 teaspoons salt
- 2½ teaspoons SAF yeast or 1 tablespoon bread machine yeast
- ²/₃ cup chopped dried sour cherries
- ¹/₃ cup slivered blanched almonds

1. Place the ingredients, except the cherries and almonds, in the pan according to the order in the manufacturer's instructions. Set crust on medium and program for the Basic or Fruit and Nut cycle; press Start. When the machine beeps, or between Knead 1 and Knead 2, add the cherries and almonds.
2. When the baking cycle ends, immediately remove the bread from the pan and place it on a rack. Let cool to room temperature before slicing.

Apricot Oat Bread

Makes 2 pounds

- 1 cup apple or pear juice
- 7 tablespoons water
- 2½ tablespoons honey
- 2½ tablespoons nut or vegetable oil
- 2¹/₃ cups bread flour
- 1 cup whole wheat flour
- ²/₃ cup rolled oats
- 1 tablespoon plus 1 teaspoon gluten
- 1½ teaspoons salt
- 2½ teaspoons SAF yeast or 1 tablespoon bread machine yeast
- ²/₃ cup finely chopped dried apricots

1. Place the ingredients, except the apricots, in the pan according to the order in the manufacturer's instructions. Set crust on medium and program for the Whole Wheat or Fruit and Nut cycle; press Start. When the machine beeps, or between Knead 1 and Knead 2, add the apricots. The dough ball will be soft and moist.
2. When the baking cycle ends, immediately remove the bread from the pan and place it on a rack. Let cool to room temperature before slicing.

Cinnamon Orange Bread

Makes 2 pounds

For the Dough:

- ⅔ cup orange juice
- ½ cup milk
- 1 large egg
- 4 tablespoons unsalted butter, cut into pieces
- 4 cups bread flour
- ⅓ cup sugar
- Grated zest of 1 orange
- 1 tablespoon plus 1 teaspoon gluten
- 2½ teaspoons ground cinnamon
- 1½ teaspoons salt
- 2¼ teaspoons SAF yeast or 2¾ teaspoons bread machine yeast

For the Vanilla-Orange Glaze:

- ¾ cup sifted confectioners' sugar
- 1½ to 2 tablespoons orange juice
- 1 teaspoon vanilla extract

1. To make the dough, place all the dough ingredients in the pan according to the order in the manufacturer's instructions. Set crust on medium and program for the Basic cycle; press Start.
2. When the baking cycle ends, immediately remove the bread from the pan and place it on a rack. Place a plate or piece of waxed paper under the rack.
3. To prepare the glaze, combine the confectioners' sugar, orange juice, and vanilla in a small bowl; beat with a small whisk until smooth. With a large spoon, drizzle the bread with the glaze, letting it drip down the sides. Cool to room temperature to set the glaze before slicing.

Pear, Fig, and Prune Bread

Makes 2 pounds

For the Dough:

- ¼ cup plus 1 tablespoon milk
- ¼ cup water
- 1 large egg
- 3 tablespoons unsalted butter, partially melted
- 2½ cups unbleached all-purpose flour
- ¼ cup sugar
- 1 teaspoon salt
- 2 teaspoons SAF yeast or 2½ teaspoons bread machine yeast

For the Fruit Filling:

- ¾ cup dry red wine
- ¼ cup kirsch
- ¼ cup sugar
- Grated zest of 1 lemon
- ½ teaspoon ground cinnamon
- ¼ teaspoon fresh-ground nutmeg
- 8 ounces (227 g) dried pears, chopped
- 6 ounces (170 g) dried figs, stemmed and chopped
- 4 ounces (113 g) pitted prunes
- ¼ cup raisins
- 1 egg yolk beaten with 1 tablespoon milk, for glaze

1. To make the dough, place all the dough ingredients in the pan according to the order in the manufacturer's instructions. Program for the Dough cycle; press Start. The dough ball will be firm, yet pliable.
2. While the dough is rising, make the filling. Combine the wine, kirsch, sugar, zest, and spices in a small saucepan and bring to a boil. Lower heat and add the dried fruit. Simmer, uncovered, for 10 minutes. Remove from the heat, cover, and let stand until room temperature and all of the liquid is absorbed, about 1 hour. Place in a food processor and pulse to make a thick jam that is not totally smooth.
3. Line a baking sheet with parchment paper. To assemble the loaf, when the machine beeps at the end of the cycle, press Stop and unplug the machine. Turn the dough out onto a lightly floured work surface. With a rolling pin, roll out into a 12-by-16-inch rectangle. With a metal spatula, spread the filling evenly over the dough, leaving ½-inch borders on three sides and a 1-inch border on one long side. Beginning at the long edge with the ½-inch border, roll up jelly-roll fashion to make a log. Moisten the 1-inch border with some water and seal. Pinch the bottom seam, leaving the ends open. Press to even the ends. Using the tines of a fork, prick the dough all over. Brush with the egg glaze. Let rest at room temperature, covered loosely with a clean tea towel, until doubled in bulk, about 45 minutes.
4. Twenty minutes before baking, preheat the oven to 350ºF (180ºC).
5. Brush the roll once more with the egg glaze. Bake for 30 to 40 minutes, until golden brown and firm to the touch. Let cool on the baking sheet.

Currant and Walnut Bread

Makes 2 pounds

- 1 1/3 cups buttermilk
- 2 large egg whites, lightly beaten
- 1/4 cup canola oil
- 2 cups bread flour
- 2 cups whole wheat flour
- 1/3 cup rolled oats
- 1/3 cup dark brown sugar
- 2 1/2 tablespoons gluten

- 2 teaspoons salt
- 1 1/2 teaspoons ground cinnamon
- 1 1/2 teaspoons vanilla powder
- 1 tablespoon SAF yeast or 1 tablespoon plus 1/2 teaspoon bread machine yeast
- 2/3 cup currants
- 1/3 cup chopped walnuts

1. Place the ingredients, except the fruit and nuts, in the pan according to the order in the manufacturer's instructions. Set crust on dark and program for the Basic or Fruit and Nut cycle; press Start. When the machine beeps, or between Knead 1 and Knead 2, add the fruit and nuts. Do not be tempted to add more than a tablespoon of extra flour. This is a moist dough ball that will initially look very sticky, especially around the blade. It will transform to tacky by the end of the kneading and be smooth and shiny with the rises.
2. When the baking cycle ends, immediately remove the bread from the pan and place it on a rack. Let cool to room temperature before slicing.

Walnut and Raisin Ricotta Bread

Makes 2 pounds

- 1/2 cup milk
- 3/4 cup ricotta cheese
- 3 large egg yolks
- 2 teaspoons anise extract
- 1/2 cup (1 stick) plus 1 tablespoon unsalted butter, cut into pieces
- 4 cups bread flour
- 1/2 cup walnuts

- 1/2 cup golden raisins
- 3 1/2 tablespoons sugar
- Grated zest of 2 lemons
- 1 tablespoon plus 1 teaspoon gluten
- 2 teaspoons salt
- 2 1/2 teaspoons SAF yeast or 1 tablespoon bread machine yeast

1. Place all the ingredients in the pan according to the order in the manufacturer's instructions. Set crust on medium and program for the Basic cycle; press Start.
2. When the baking cycle ends, immediately remove the bread from the pan and place it on a rack. Let cool to room temperature before slicing.

Greek Currant and Orange Bread

Makes 2 pounds

- 1 ¹/₃ cups currants
- ¼ cup orange juice
- One 2-inch piece cinnamon stick
- 2 whole cloves
- Pinch of ground mastika or allspice
- 1 ⅛ cups plus 1 tablespoon evaporated milk
- 2 teaspoons orange-flower water
- ¼ cup honey
- 4 cups bread flour
- 1 tablespoon plus
- 1 teaspoon gluten
- 2 teaspoons salt
- 2½ teaspoons SAF yeast or 1 tablespoon bread machine yeast

1. Place the currants in a small bowl. Add the orange juice, cinnamon stick, cloves, and mastika or allspice. Toss to combine. Cover and let stand at room temperature for 1 hour. The currants will be soft and plump. Remove and discard the cinnamon stick and cloves.
2. Drain and reserve any extra orange juice from the currants. Add 3 tablespoons water to the juice.
3. Place the ingredients, except the currants, in the pan according to the order in the manufacturer's instructions, adding the juice and water mixture with the liquid ingredients. Set crust on medium and program for the Sweet Bread or Fruit and Nut cycle; press Start. When the machine beeps, or between Knead 1 and Knead 2, add the currants.
4. When the baking cycle ends, immediately remove the bread from the pan and place it on a rack. Let cool to room temperature before slicing.

Dutch Cinnamon Loaf

Makes 2 pounds

- ¾ cup sugar cubes
- 2 teaspoons ground cinnamon
- Small pinch of ground cloves
- 1 ¹/₃ cups fat-free milk
- 2 tablespoons unsalted butter or margarine, cut into pieces
- 4 cups bread flour
- 1 tablespoon plus 1 teaspoon gluten
- 1¾ teaspoons salt
- 2½ teaspoons SAF yeast or 1 tablespoon bread machine yeast

1. Place the sugar cubes in a heavy clear plastic freezer bag and, using the smooth side of a meat hammer, crack the cubes. Don't crush them; you want the chunks to be no smaller than quarter cubes, if possible. Add the spices to the bag and toss to coat. Set aside.

2. Place the ingredients, except the spice-coated sugar cubes, in the pan according to the order in the manufacturer's instructions. Set crust on medium, and program for the Sweet Bread cycle; press Start. 5 minutes into the kneading segment, press Pause and sprinkle in half of the sugar cube mixture. Press Start to resume the cycle. 3 minutes later, press Pause and add the rest of the sugar cube mixture. Press Start to resume the cycle.
3. When the baking cycle ends, immediately remove the bread from the pan and place it on a rack. Let cool to room temperature before slicing, or sugar syrup will ooze out.

Rum Persimmon Bread with Golden Raisins

Makes 2 pounds

- 2 large Hachiya persimmons
- 1 cup milk
- 1 large egg
- 1½ tablespoons amber rum
- 3 tablespoons butter, cut into pieces
- 4 cups bread flour

- 3 tablespoons dark brown sugar
- 1 tablespoon gluten
- 2 teaspoons apple pie spice
- 2 teaspoons salt
- 2½ teaspoons SAF yeast or 1 tablespoon bread machine yeast
- 1 cup golden raisins

1. Cut the soft persimmons in half and scoop out the inner flesh with a large spoon. Measure out and reserve ¾ cup for the loaf.
2. Place the ingredients, except the raisins, in the pan according to the order in the manufacturer's instructions, adding the reserved persimmon pulp with the liquid ingredients. Set crust on dark and program for the Basic or Fruit and Nut cycle; press Start. When the machine beeps, or between Knead 1 and Knead 2, add the raisins. The dough ball will be soft and springy.
3. When the baking cycle ends, immediately remove the bread from the pan and place it on a rack. Let cool to room temperature before slicing. The bread is very tender, so be sure not to cut it before it cools.

Whole-Wheat Breads

Chapter 3

Basic Whole Wheat Bread

- ½ cup lukewarm whole milk
- 2 tablespoons unsalted butter, diced
- 1 cup whole wheat flour
- 1 cup pain bread flour
- 2½ tablespoons brown sugar
- ¾ teaspoon salt
- ¾ teaspoon bread machine yeast

1. Add the ingredients into the bread machine as per the order of the ingredients listed above or follow your bread machine's instruction manual.
2. Select the Whole Wheat cycle and medium crust function.
3. When ready, turn the bread out onto a drying rack and allow it to cool, then serve.

Authentic Whole Wheat Challah

- 1 cup water
- 3 large eggs
- ¼ cup vegetable oil
- 2½ tablespoons honey
- 2 cups whole wheat flour
- 2 cups bread flour
- 2 tablespoons gluten
- 1¼ tablespoons instant potato flakes
- 2 teaspoons salt
- 2½ teaspoons SAF yeast or 1 tablespoon bread machine yeast

1. Place all the ingredients in the pan according to the order in the manufacturer's instructions. Set crust on medium or dark, and program for the Basic or Whole Wheat cycle; press Start. This is a moist dough ball. Do not add more flour during the kneading or the bread will be dry.
2. When Rise 2 ends, press Pause, open the lid and lift the warm dough from the pan. Divide the dough into 2 equal portions. With the palms of your hands, roll each portion into a fat oblong sausage, about 10 inches long. Place the two pieces side by side. Holding each end, wrap one around the other, twisting each one at the same time, to create a fat twist effect. Tuck under the ends and replace in the pan in the machine. The twist shape will bake in the machine.
3. When the baking cycle ends, immediately remove the bread from the pan and place it on a rack. Let cool to room temperature before slicing.

Potato Whole Wheat Bread

Makes 2 pounds

- 1²/₃ cups water
- 4 tablespoons butter, cut into pieces
- 3 tablespoons honey
- 2½ cups whole wheat flour
- 1½ cups bread flour
- ¹/₃ cup instant potato flakes
- 2 tablespoons gluten
- 2 teaspoons salt
- 2½ teaspoons SAF yeast or 1 tablespoon bread machine yeast

1. Place all the ingredients in the pan according to the order in the manufacturer's instructions. Set crust on medium and program for the Whole Wheat cycle; press Start.
2. When the baking cycle ends, immediately remove the bread from the pan and place it on a rack. Let cool to room temperature before slicing.

Whole Wheat Flax Seed Bread

Makes 2 pounds

- 1½ cups water
- 3 tablespoons canola oil
- ¼ cup honey
- 2²/₃ cups bread flour
- 1¹/₃ cups whole wheat flour
- ¹/₃ cup nonfat dry milk
- 2½ tablespoons flax seed
- 1¼ tablespoons gluten
- 1½ teaspoons salt
- 2¼ teaspoons SAF yeast or 2¾ teaspoons bread machine yeast

1. Place all the ingredients in the pan according to the order in the manufacturer's instructions. Set crust on medium and program for the Basic or Whole Wheat cycle; press Start.
2. When the baking cycle ends, immediately remove the bread from the pan and place it on a rack. Let cool to room temperature before slicing.

Classic Dakota Bread

Makes 2 pounds

- 1½ cups water
- 3 tablespoons canola oil
- 3 tablespoons honey
- 21 cups bread flour
- 1 cup whole wheat flour
- ⅓ cup raw bulgur cracked wheat
- 1 tablespoon gluten
- 2 teaspoons salt
- ⅓ cup raw sunflower seeds
- ⅓ cup raw pumpkin seeds, chopped
- 2 teaspoons sesame seeds
- 2 teaspoons poppy seeds
- 2¼ teaspoons SAF yeast or 2¾ teaspoons bread machine yeast

1. Place all the ingredients in the pan according to the order in the manufacturer's instructions. Set crust on dark and program for the Basic cycle; press Start.
2. When the baking cycle ends, immediately remove the bread from the pan and place it on a rack. Let cool to room temperature before slicing.

Whole Wheat Buttermilk Bread

Makes 2 pounds

- 1½ cups buttermilk
- 3 tablespoons canola oil
- 2½ tablespoons maple syrup
- 2 cups whole wheat flour
- 2 cups bread flour
- 1 tablespoon plus 2 teaspoons gluten
- 2 teaspoons salt
- 2¼ teaspoons SAF yeast or 2¾ teaspoons bread machine yeast

1. Place all the ingredients in the pan according to the order in the manufacturer's instructions. Set crust on medium and program for the Basic or Whole Wheat cycle; press Start.
2. When the baking cycle ends, immediately remove the bread from the pan and place it on a rack. Let cool to room temperature before slicing.

Orange Whole Wheat Bread

Makes 2 pounds

- Zest of 2 oranges, cut into very thin strips
- 1²/₃ cups fat-free milk
- 3 tablespoons olive or walnut oil
- 3 tablespoons honey
- 2¼ cups whole wheat flour
- 2 cups bread flour
- 1 tablespoon plus 1 teaspoon gluten
- 1½ teaspoons salt
- 2¼ teaspoons SAF yeast or 2¾ teaspoons bread machine yeast

1. In a food processor, chop the orange peel fine, or chop it fine by hand.
2. Place all the ingredients in the pan according to the order in the manufacturer's instructions. Set crust on medium and program for the Whole Wheat cycle; press Start.
3. When the baking cycle ends, immediately remove the bread from the pan and place it on a rack. Let cool to room temperature before slicing.

Multi-Seed Whole Wheat Bread

Makes 1 pound

- ²/₃ cups lukewarm water
- 3 tablespoons milk powder
- 1 tablespoon honey
- 1 tablespoon unsalted butter, softened
- 1 cup plain bread flour
- 1 cup whole wheat flour
- 2 tablespoons poppy seeds
- 2 tablespoons sesame seeds
- 2 tablespoons sunflower seeds
- ¾ teaspoon salt
- 2 teaspoons instant dry yeast

1. Add the ingredients into the bread machine as per the order of the ingredients listed above or follow your bread machine's instruction manual.
2. Select the Basic cycle and medium crust function.
3. When ready, turn the bread out onto a drying rack and allow it to cool, then serve.

Oatmeal and Honey Whole Wheat Bread

Makes 1 pound

- ²/₃ cup lukewarm water
- ½ tablespoon olive oil
- 8 teaspoons honey
- ½ cup rolled oats
- ¾ cup whole wheat flour
- ¾ cup white bread flour
- ½ teaspoon salt
- ½ teaspoon instant yeast

1. All ingredients should enter your bread machine either in the order listed or according to your bread machine's instruction manual.
2. Select the Basic cycle and soft crust function.
3. When ready, turn the bread out onto a drying rack so it can cool, then serve.

Whole Wheat Graham Bread

Makes 2 pounds

- 1¹/₃ cups water
- 1 large egg plus 1 egg yolk
- 3 tablespoons butter, cut into pieces
- 3 cups bread flour
- 1 cup graham flour
- ½ cup nonfat dry milk
- ¹/₃ cup light brown sugar
- 1 tablespoon gluten
- 2 teaspoons salt
- 2¼ teaspoons SAF yeast or 2¾ teaspoons bread machine yeast

1. Place all the ingredients in the pan according to the order in the manufacturer's instructions. Set crust on medium and program for the Basic or Whole Wheat cycle; press Start.
2. When the baking cycle ends, immediately remove the bread from the pan and place it on a rack. Let cool to room temperature before slicing.

Simple Cracked Wheat Bread

Makes 2 pounds

- 1 cup boiling water
- ²/₃ cup cracked wheat or bulgur
- ¼ cup molasses
- 3 tablespoons unsalted butter or margarine, cut into pieces
- 2 teaspoons salt
- 1 cup water

- 3½ cups bread flour
- ½ cup whole wheat flour
- 1 tablespoon plus 1 teaspoon gluten
- 1 tablespoon SAF yeast or 1 tablespoon plus ½ teaspoon bread machine yeast

1. Pour the boiling water over the cracked wheat in a bowl. Add the molasses, butter, and salt. Let stand 1 hour at room temperature to soften.
2. Place the ingredients in the pan according to the order in the manufacturer's instructions, adding the cracked wheat mixture and the additional water as the liquid ingredients. Set crust on medium and program for the Basic cycle; press Start.
3. When the baking cycle ends, immediately remove the bread from the pan and place it on a rack. Let cool to room temperature before slicing.

Honey Whole Wheat Bread

Makes 1 pound

- 1⅛ cups lukewarm water
- 3 tablespoons honey
- 2 tablespoons vegetable oil
- 1½ cups plain bread flour

- 1½ cups whole wheat flour
- ¹/₃ teaspoon salt
- 1½ teaspoons instant dry yeast

1. Add the ingredients into the bread machine as per the order of the ingredients listed above or follow your bread machine's instruction manual.
2. Select the Whole Wheat cycle and medium crust function.
3. When ready, turn the bread out onto a drying rack and allow it to cool, then serve.

Whole Wheat Seed Bread

Makes 1 pound

- ²/₃ cup lukewarm water
- 1 tablespoon olive oil
- 2 tablespoons maple syrup
- 1¾ cups white whole wheat flour
- 6 teaspoons assorted seeds (an even mix of flax, sesame and/ or sunflower seeds)
- ¾ teaspoon salt
- ¾ teaspoon instant yeast

1. Place all ingredients into your bread machine in the exact order listed.
2. Select the whole-wheat setting and the medium crust function.
3. When ready, turn the bread out onto a drying rack so it can cool, then serve.

Super Whole Wheat Bread

Makes 1 pound

- 1 cup lukewarm water
- 1¼ tablespoons milk powder
- 1¼ tablespoons unsalted butter, diced
- 1¼ tablespoons honey
- 1¼ tablespoons molasses
- 1 teaspoon salt
- 2¼ cups whole wheat flour
- 1 teaspoon active dry yeast

1. Add the ingredients into the bread machine as per the order of the ingredients listed above or follow your bread machine's instruction manual.
2. Select the Whole Wheat cycle and medium crust function.
3. When ready, turn the bread out onto a drying rack and allow it to cool, then serve.

Sour-Honey Whole Wheat Dinner Rolls

Makes 16 dinner rolls

- ²/₃ cup milk
- ½ cup sour cream
- ¼ cup honey
- 2 large eggs
- 4 tablespoons butter or margarine, cut into pieces
- 3 cups unbleached all-purpose flour
- 1 cup whole wheat flour
- ½ cup toasted wheat germ
- 1½ teaspoons salt
- 2 teaspoons SAF yeast or 2½ teaspoons bread machine yeast

1. Place all the ingredients in the pan according to the order in the manufacturer's instructions. Program for the Dough cycle; press Start.
2. Grease a large baking sheet or line with parchment paper. When the machine beeps at the end of the cycle, press Stop and unplug the machine. Turn the dough out onto a lightly floured surface. Divide the dough in half, then roll each half into a 2- to 3-inch cylinder. With a metal dough scraper or a chef's knife, cut the cylinder into 8 equal portions. Repeat with the second cylinder, making a total of 16 equal portions. Shape each portion like a miniature loaf by patting it into an oval, then rolling up from a short side to make a small compact cylinder about 4 inches long. Place the rolls in two rows of 8 with their long sides touching. Brush some melted butter on the tops of the rolls. Cover loosely with plastic wrap and let rise at room temperature until doubled in bulk, about 45 minutes.
3. 20 minutes before baking, preheat the oven to 375ºF (190ºC).
4. Place the baking sheet in the center of the oven and bake for 25 minutes, until golden brown. Remove the rolls from the pans and let cool on a rack. Serve warm, or cool to room temperature and reheat before serving.

Cheese Breads

Chapter 4

Chipotle Cheese Bread

Makes 1 pound

- ²/₃ cup water, at 80ºF (27ºC) to 90ºF (32ºC)
- 1½ tablespoons sugar
- 1½ tablespoons powdered skim milk
- ¾ teaspoon salt
- ½ teaspoon chipotle chili powder
- 2 cups white bread flour
- ½ cup shredded sharp Cheddar cheese
- ¾ teaspoon bread machine or instant yeast

1. Place the ingredients in your bread machine as recommended by the manufacturer.
2. Set the machine to Basic cycle, select light or medium crust, and press Start.
3. When the loaf is done, remove the bucket from the machine.
4. Let the loaf cool for 5 minutes.
5. Gently shake the bucket to remove the loaf, and turn it out onto a rack to cool.

Cheesy Black Olive Swiss Bread

Makes 1 pound

- ²/₃ cup milk, at 80ºF (27ºC) to 90ºF (32ºC)
- 1 tablespoon melted butter, cooled
- ²/₃ teaspoon minced garlic
- 1 tablespoon sugar
- ²/₃ teaspoon salt
- 2 cups white bread flour
- ½ cup shredded Swiss cheese
- ¾ teaspoon bread machine or instant yeast
- ¼ cup chopped black olives

1. Place the ingredients in your bread machine as recommended by the manufacturer, tossing the flour with the cheese first.
2. Set the machine to Basic cycle, select light or medium crust, and press Start.
3. When the loaf is done, remove the bucket from the machine.
4. Let the loaf cool for 5 minutes.
5. Gently shake the bucket to remove the loaf, and turn it out onto a rack to cool.

Asiago Cheese Bread

Makes 1 pound

- ½ cup plus 1 tablespoon milk, at 70ºF (21ºC) to 80ºF (27ºC)
- 2²/₃ tablespoons melted butter, cooled
- ²/₃ teaspoon minced garlic
- 4 teaspoons sugar
- ²/₃ teaspoon salt
- ¹/₃ cup grated Asiago cheese
- 1¾ cups plus 1 tablespoon white bread flour
- 1 teaspoon bread machine or instant yeast
- ¹/₃ cup mashed roasted garlic

1. Place the ingredients, except the roasted garlic, in your bread machine as recommended by the manufacturer.
2. Set the machine to Basic cycle, select light or medium crust, and press Start.
3. Add the roasted garlic when your machine signals or 5 minutes before the last kneading is done.
4. When the loaf is done, remove the bucket from the machine.
5. Let the loaf cool for 5 minutes.
6. Gently shake the bucket to remove the loaf, and turn it out onto a rack to cool.

Oregano Feta Cheese Bread

Makes 1 pound

- ²/₃ cup milk, at 80ºF (27ºC) to 90ºF (32ºC)
- 2 teaspoons melted butter, cooled
- 2 teaspoons sugar
- ²/₃ teaspoon salt
- 2 teaspoons dried oregano
- 2 cups white bread flour
- 1½ teaspoons bread machine or instant yeast
- ²/₃ cup crumbled feta cheese

1. Place the ingredients in your bread machine as recommended by the manufacturer.
2. Set the machine to Basic cycle, select light or medium crust, and press Start.
3. When the loaf is done, remove the bucket from the machine.
4. Let the loaf cool for 5 minutes.
5. Gently shake the bucket to remove the loaf, and turn it out onto a rack to cool.

Cottage Cheese Bread

Makes 1 pound

- $^1/_3$ cup water, at 80ºF (27ºC) to 90ºF (32ºC)
- ½ cup low-fat cottage cheese, at room temperature
- 1 egg, at room temperature
- 4 teaspoons butter, melted and cooled
- 2 teaspoons sugar
- $^2/_3$ teaspoon salt
- ⅛ teaspoon baking soda
- 2 cups white bread flour
- 1$^1/_3$ teaspoons bread machine or instant yeast

1. Place the ingredients in your bread machine as recommended by the manufacturer.
2. Set the machine to Basic cycle, select light or medium crust, and press Start.
3. When the loaf is done, remove the bucket from the machine.
4. Let the loaf cool for 5 minutes.
5. Gently shake the bucket to remove the loaf, and turn it out onto a rack to cool.

Basil Cheddar Bread

Makes 1 pound

- $^2/_3$ cup milk, at 80ºF (27ºC) to 90ºF (32ºC)
- 2 teaspoons melted butter, cooled
- 2 teaspoons sugar
- $^2/_3$ teaspoon dried basil
- ½ cup shredded sharp Cheddar cheese
- ½ teaspoon salt
- 2 cups white bread flour
- 1 teaspoon bread machine or active dry yeast

1. Place the ingredients in your bread machine as recommended by the manufacturer.
2. Set the machine to Basic cycle, select light or medium crust, and press Start.
3. When the loaf is done, remove the bucket from the machine.
4. Let the loaf cool for 5 minutes.
5. Gently shake the bucket to remove the loaf, and turn it out onto a rack to cool.

Herbed Mozzarella Cheese Bread

Makes 1 pound

- ¾ cup plus 1 tablespoon milk, at 80ºF (27ºC) to 90ºF (32ºC)
- 2 teaspoons butter, melted and cooled
- 4 teaspoons sugar
- ²/₃ teaspoon salt
- 1¹/₃ teaspoons dried basil
- ²/₃ teaspoon dried oregano
- 1 cup shredded mozzarella cheese
- 2 cups white bread flour
- 1½ teaspoons bread machine or instant yeast

1. Place the ingredients in your bread machine as recommended by the manufacturer.
2. Set the machine to Basic cycle, select light or medium crust, and press Start.
3. When the loaf is done, remove the bucket from the machine.
4. Let the loaf cool for 5 minutes.
5. Gently shake the bucket to remove the loaf, and turn it out onto a rack to cool.

Aged Cheddar Cheese Bread

Makes 1 pound

- ²/₃ cup milk, at 80ºF (27ºC) to 90ºF (32ºC)
- 4 teaspoons butter, melted and cooled
- 2 tablespoons sugar
- ²/₃ teaspoon salt
- ¹/₃ cup grated aged Cheddar cheese
- 2 cups white bread flour
- 1¹/₃ teaspoons bread machine or instant yeast

1. Place the ingredients in your bread machine as recommended by the manufacturer.
2. Set the machine to Basic cycle, select light or medium crust, and press Start.
3. When the loaf is done, remove the bucket from the machine.
4. Let the loaf cool for 5 minutes.
5. Gently shake the bucket to remove the loaf, and turn it out onto a rack to cool.

Blue Cheese Bread with Potato Flakes

- ¾ cup plus 1 tablespoon water, at 80ºF (27ºC) to 90ºF (32ºC)
- 1 egg, at room temperature
- 2 teaspoons melted butter, cooled
- 3 tablespoons powdered skim milk
- 2 teaspoons sugar
- ½ teaspoon salt
- $^1/_3$ cup crumbled blue cheese
- 2 teaspoons dried onion flakes
- 2 cups white bread flour
- 3 tablespoons instant mashed potato flakes
- ¾ teaspoon bread machine or active dry yeast

1. Place the ingredients in your bread machine as recommended by the manufacturer.
2. Set the machine to Basic cycle, select light or medium crust, and press Start.
3. When the loaf is done, remove the bucket from the machine.
4. Let the loaf cool for 5 minutes.
5. Gently shake the bucket to remove the loaf, and turn it out onto a rack to cool.

Cheddar and Parmesan Cheese Bread

- ¾ cup plus 1 tablespoon milk, at 80ºF (27ºC) to 90ºF (32ºC)
- 2 teaspoons butter, melted and cooled
- 4 teaspoons sugar
- $^2/_3$ teaspoon salt
- $^1/_3$ teaspoon freshly ground black pepper
- Pinch cayenne pepper
- 1 cup shredded aged sharp Cheddar cheese
- $^1/_3$ cup shredded or grated Parmesan cheese
- 2 cups white bread flour
- ¾ teaspoon bread machine or instant yeast

1. Place the ingredients in your bread machine as recommended by the manufacturer.
2. Set the machine to Basic cycle, select light or medium crust, and press Start.
3. When the loaf is done, remove the bucket from the machine.
4. Let the loaf cool for 5 minutes.
5. Gently shake the bucket to remove the loaf, and turn it out onto a rack to cool.

Salami and Mozzarella Cheese Bread

Makes 1 pound

- ¾ cup water, at 80ºF (27ºC) to 90ºF (32ºC)
- ⅓ cup shredded mozzarella cheese
- 4 teaspoons sugar
- ⅔ teaspoon salt
- ⅔ teaspoon dried basil
- Pinch garlic powder
- 2 cups plus 2 tablespoons white bread flour
- 1 teaspoon bread machine or instant yeast
- ½ cup finely diced hot German salami

1. Place the ingredients, except the salami, in your bread machine as recommended by the manufacturer.
2. Set the machine to Basic cycle, select light or medium crust, and press Start.
3. Add the salami when your machine signals or 5 minutes before the second Kneading cycle is finished.
4. When the loaf is done, remove the bucket from the machine.
5. Let the loaf cool for 5 minutes.
6. Gently shake the bucket to remove the loaf, and turn it out onto a rack to cool.

Chile-Bacon Cheddar Bread

Makes 1 pound

- ⅓ cup milk, at 80ºF (27ºC) to 90ºF (32ºC)
- 1 teaspoon melted butter, cooled
- 1 tablespoon honey
- 1 teaspoon salt
- ⅓ cup chopped and drained green chiles
- ⅓ cup grated Cheddar cheese
- ⅓ cup chopped cooked bacon
- 2 cups white bread flour
- 1⅓ teaspoons bread machine or instant yeast

1. Place the ingredients in your bread machine as recommended by the manufacturer.
2. Set the machine to Basic cycle, select light or medium crust, and press Start.
3. When the loaf is done, remove the bucket from the machine.
4. Let the loaf cool for 5 minutes.
5. Gently shake the bucket to remove the loaf, and turn it out onto a rack to cool.

Italian Parmesan Cheese White Bread

Makes 1 pound

- ¾ cup water, at 80ºF (27ºC) to 90ºF (32ºC)
- 2 tablespoons melted butter, cooled
- 2 teaspoons sugar
- ⅔ teaspoon salt

- 1⅓ teaspoons chopped fresh basil
- 2⅔ tablespoons grated Parmesan cheese
- 2⅓ cups white bread flour
- 1 teaspoon bread machine or instant yeast

1. Place the ingredients in your bread machine as recommended by the manufacturer.
2. Set the machine to Basic cycle, select light or medium crust, and press Start.
3. When the loaf is done, remove the bucket from the machine.
4. Let the loaf cool for 5 minutes.
5. Gently shake the bucket to remove the loaf, and turn it out onto a rack to cool.

Easy Goat Cheese Bread

Makes 1 pound

- ⅔ cup milk, at 80ºF (27ºC) to 90ºF (32ºC)
- 2⅔ tablespoons goat cheese, at room temperature
- 1 tablespoon honey
- ⅔ teaspoon salt

- ⅔ teaspoon freshly cracked black pepper
- 2 cups white bread flour
- 1 teaspoon bread machine or instant yeast

1. Place the ingredients in your bread machine as recommended by the manufacturer.
2. Set the machine to Basic cycle, select light or medium crust, and press Start.
3. When the loaf is done, remove the bucket from the machine.
4. Let the loaf cool for 5 minutes.
5. Gently shake the bucket to remove the loaf, and turn it out onto a rack to cool.

Corn-Jalapeño Cheddar Bread

Makes 1½ to 2 pounds

- 1 cup buttermilk, at 80ºF (27ºC) to 90ºF (32ºC)
- ¼ cup melted butter, cooled
- 2 eggs, at room temperature
- 1 jalapeño pepper, chopped
- 1⅓ cups all-purpose flour
- 1 cup cornmeal
- ½ cup shredded Cheddar cheese
- ¼ cup sugar
- 1 tablespoon baking powder
- ½ teaspoon salt

1. Place the buttermilk, butter, eggs, and jalapeño pepper in your bread machine.
2. Program the machine for Quick cycle and press Start.
3. While the wet ingredients are mixing, stir together the flour, cornmeal, cheese, sugar, baking powder, and salt in a small bowl.
4. After the first fast mixing is done and the machine signals, add the dry ingredients.
5. When the loaf is done, remove the bucket from the machine.
6. Let the loaf cool for 5 minutes.
7. Gently shake the bucket to remove the loaf, and turn it out onto a rack to cool.

Fruit Breads

Chapter
5

Orange Bread

Makes 1 pound

- 1¼ cups milk, at 80ºF (27ºC) to 90ºF (32ºC)
- 2 tablespoons freshly squeezed orange juice, at room temperature
- 2 tablespoons sugar
- ¾ tablespoon melted butter, cooled
- ¾ teaspoon salt
- 2 cups white bread flour
- Zest of ½ orange
- 1 teaspoon bread machine or instant yeast

1. Place the ingredients in your bread machine as recommended by the manufacturer.
2. Set the machine to Basic cycle, select light or medium crust, and press Start.
3. When the loaf is done, remove the bucket from the machine.
4. Let the loaf cool for 5 minutes.
5. Gently shake the bucket to remove the loaf, and turn it out onto a rack to cool.

Cinnamon Oat Apple Bread

Makes 1 pound

- ½ cup milk, at 80ºF (27ºC) to 90ºF (32ºC)
- 2¾ tablespoons unsweetened applesauce, at room temperature
- 2 teaspoons melted butter, cooled
- 2 teaspoons sugar
- $2/_3$ teaspoon salt
- ¼ teaspoon ground cinnamon
- Pinch ground nutmeg
- 2¾ tablespoons quick oats
- 1½ cups white bread flour
- 1½ teaspoons bread machine or active dry yeast

1. Place the ingredients in your bread machine as recommended by the manufacturer.
2. Set the machine to Basic cycle, select light or medium crust, and press Start.
3. When the loaf is done, remove the bucket from the machine.
4. Let the loaf cool for 5 minutes.
5. Gently shake the bucket to remove the loaf, and turn it out onto a rack to cool.

Oat Shortcake Strawberry Bread

Makes 1 pound

- ¾ cup milk, at 80ºF (27ºC) to 90ºF (32ºC)
- 2 tablespoons melted butter, cooled
- 2 tablespoons sugar
- 1 teaspoon salt
- ½ cup sliced fresh strawberries
- ¾ cup quick oats
- 1½ cups white bread flour
- 1 teaspoon bread machine or instant yeast

1. Place the ingredients in your bread machine as recommended by the manufacturer.
2. Set the machine to Basic cycle, select light or medium crust, and press Start.
3. When the loaf is done, remove the bucket from the machine.
4. Let the loaf cool for 5 minutes.
5. Gently shake the bucket to remove the loaf, and turn it out onto a rack to cool.

Citrus Blueberry Bread

Makes 1 pound

- ½ cup plain yogurt, at room temperature
- $1/_3$ cup water, at 80ºF (27ºC) to 90ºF (32ºC)
- 2 tablespoons honey
- 2 teaspoons melted butter, cooled
- 1 teaspoon salt
- $1/_3$ teaspoon lemon extract
- 1 teaspoon lime zest
- $2/_3$ cup dried blueberries
- 2 cups white bread flour
- 1½ teaspoons bread machine or instant yeast

1. Place the ingredients in your bread machine as recommended by the manufacturer.
2. Set the machine to Basic cycle, select light or medium crust, and press Start.
3. When the loaf is done, remove the bucket from the machine.
4. Let the loaf cool for 5 minutes.
5. Gently shake the bucket to remove the loaf, and turn it out onto a rack to cool.

Coconut Pineapple Bread

Makes 1½ to 2 pounds

- 6 tablespoons butter, at room temperature
- 2 eggs, at room temperature
- ½ cup coconut milk, at room temperature
- ½ cup pineapple juice, at room temperature
- 1 cup sugar
- 1½ teaspoons coconut extract
- 2 cups all-purpose flour
- ¾ cup shredded sweetened coconut
- 1 teaspoon baking powder
- ½ teaspoon salt

1. Place the butter, eggs, coconut milk, pineapple juice, sugar, and coconut extract in your bread machine.
2. Program the machine for Quick cycle and press Start.
3. While the wet ingredients are mixing, stir together the flour, coconut, baking powder, and salt in a small bowl.
4. After the first fast mixing is done and the machine signals, add the dry ingredients.
5. When the loaf is done, remove the bucket from the machine.
6. Let the loaf cool for 5 minutes.
7. Gently shake the bucket to remove the loaf, and turn it out onto a rack to cool.

Fast and Easy Black Olive Bread

Makes 1 pound

- $^2/_3$ cup milk, at 80ºF (27ºC) to 90ºF (32ºC)
- 1 tablespoon melted butter, cooled
- $^2/_3$ teaspoon minced garlic
- 1 tablespoon sugar
- $^2/_3$ teaspoon salt
- 2 cups white bread flour
- ¾ teaspoon bread machine or instant yeast
- ¼ cup chopped black olives

1. Place the ingredients in your bread machine as recommended by the manufacturer.
2. Set the machine to Basic cycle, select light or medium crust, and press Start.
3. When the loaf is done, remove the bucket from the machine.
4. Let the loaf cool for 5 minutes.
5. Gently shake the bucket to remove the loaf, and turn it out onto a rack to cool.

Cinnamon Apple Bread

Makes 1 pound

- ²/₃ cup milk, at 80ºF (27ºC) to 90ºF (32ºC)
- 1²/₃ tablespoons melted butter, cooled
- 4 teaspoons sugar
- 1 teaspoon salt
- ²/₃ teaspoon ground cinnamon
- Pinch ground cloves
- 2 cups white bread flour
- 1½ teaspoons bread machine or active dry yeast
- ²/₃ cup finely diced peeled apple

1. Place the ingredients, except the apple, in your bread machine as recommended by the manufacturer.
2. Set the machine to Basic cycle, select light or medium crust, and press Start.
3. When the machine signals, add the apple to the bucket, or add it just before the end of the second Kneading cycle if your machine does not have a signal.
4. When the loaf is done, remove the bucket from the machine.
5. Let the loaf cool for 5 minutes.
6. Gently shake the bucket to remove the loaf, and turn it out onto a rack to cool.

Whole-Wheat Banana Bread

Makes 1 pound

- ¹/₃ cup milk, at 80ºF (27ºC) to 90ºF (32ºC)
- ²/₃ cup mashed banana
- 1 egg, at room temperature
- 1 tablespoon melted butter, cooled
- 2 tablespoons honey
- ²/₃ teaspoon pure vanilla extract
- ¹/₃ teaspoon salt
- ²/₃ cup whole-wheat flour
- ¾ cup plus 1 tablespoon white bread flour
- 1 teaspoon bread machine or instant yeast

1. Place the ingredients in your bread machine as recommended by the manufacturer.
2. Program the machine for Sweet bread and press Start.
3. When the loaf is done, remove the bucket from the machine.
4. Let the loaf cool for 5 minutes.
5. Gently shake the bucket to remove the loaf, and turn it out onto a rack to cool.

Cinnamon Orange Bread with Plum

Makes 1 pound

- ¾ cup water, at 80ºF (27ºC) to 90ºF (32ºC)
- 1½ tablespoons melted butter, cooled
- 2 tablespoons sugar
- ½ teaspoon salt
- ½ teaspoon orange zest
- ¼ teaspoon ground cinnamon
- Pinch ground nutmeg
- 1¼ cups whole-wheat flour
- ¾ cup white bread flour
- 1 teaspoon bread machine or instant yeast
- ¾ cup chopped fresh plums

1. Place the ingredients, except the plums, in your bread machine as recommended by the manufacturer.
2. Set the machine to Basic cycle, select light or medium crust, and press Start.
3. When the machine signals, add the chopped plums.
4. When the loaf is done, remove the bucket from the machine.
5. Let the loaf cool for 5 minutes.
6. Gently shake the bucket to remove the loaf, and turn it out onto a rack to cool.

Creamy Peach Bread

Makes 1 pound

- ½ cup canned peaches, drained and chopped
- ¼ cup heavy whipping cream, at 80ºF (27ºC) to 90ºF (32ºC)
- 1 egg, at room temperature
- ¾ tablespoon melted butter, cooled
- 1½ tablespoons sugar
- ¾ teaspoon salt
- ¼ teaspoon ground cinnamon
- ⅛ teaspoon ground nutmeg
- ¼ cup whole-wheat flour
- 1¾ cups white bread flour
- ¾ teaspoons bread machine or instant yeast

1. Place the ingredients in your bread machine as recommended by the manufacturer.
2. Set the machine to Basic cycle, select light or medium crust, and press Start.
3. When the loaf is done, remove the bucket from the machine.
4. Let the loaf cool for 5 minutes.
5. Gently shake the bucket to remove the loaf, and turn it out onto a rack to cool.

Cranberry Orange Bread

Makes 1½ to 2 pounds

- ¾ cup milk, at 80ºF (27ºC) to 90ºF (32ºC)
- ¾ cup sugar
- ²/₃ cup melted butter, cooled
- 2 eggs, at room temperature
- ¼ cup freshly squeezed orange juice, at room temperature
- 1 tablespoon orange zest
- 1 teaspoon pure vanilla extract
- 2¼ cups all-purpose flour
- 1 cup sweetened dried cranberries
- 1½ teaspoons baking powder
- ½ teaspoon baking soda
- ½ teaspoon salt
- ¼ teaspoon ground nutmeg

1. Place the milk, sugar, butter, eggs, orange juice, zest, and vanilla in your bread machine.
2. Program the machine for Quick cycle and press Start.
3. While the wet ingredients are mixing, stir together the flour, cranberries, baking powder, baking soda, salt, and nutmeg in a medium bowl.
4. After the first fast mixing is done and the machine signals, add the dry ingredients.
5. When the loaf is done, remove the bucket from the machine.
6. Let the loaf cool for 5 minutes.
7. Gently shake the bucket to remove the loaf, and turn it out onto a rack to cool.

Whole Wheat Date Bread

Makes 1 pound

- ½ cup water, at 80ºF (27ºC) to 90ºF (32ºC)
- ½ cup milk, at 80ºF (27ºC)
- 1½ tablespoons melted butter, cooled
- 3 tablespoons honey
- 2 tablespoons molasses
- 1½ teaspoons sugar
- 1 tablespoon skim milk powder
- ½ teaspoon salt
- 1½ cups whole-wheat flour
- 1 cup white bread flour
- 2 teaspoons unsweetened cocoa powder
- 1 teaspoon bread machine or instant yeast
- ½ cup chopped dates

1. Place the ingredients, except the dates, in your bread machine as recommended by the manufacturer.

2. Set the machine to Basic cycle, select light or medium crust, and press Start.
3. When the machine signals, add the chopped dates, or put them in the nut/raisin hopper and let the machine add them automatically.
4. When the loaf is done, remove the bucket from the machine.
5. Let the loaf cool for 5 minutes.
6. Gently shake the bucket to remove the loaf, and turn it out onto a rack to cool.

Oat Blueberry Bread

Makes 1 pound

- $1/3$ cup milk, at 80°F (27°C) to 90°F (32°C)
- 1 egg, at room temperature
- $1\frac{1}{2}$ tablespoons melted butter, cooled
- 1 tablespoon honey
- $1/3$ cup rolled oats
- 2 cups white bread flour
- ¾ teaspoon salt
- 1 teaspoon bread machine or instant yeast
- $1/3$ cup dried blueberries

1. Place the ingredients, except the blueberries, in your bread machine as recommended by the manufacturer.
2. Set the machine to Basic cycle, select light or medium crust, and press Start.
3. Add the blueberries when the machine signals or 5 minutes before the second Kneading cycle is finished.
4. When the loaf is done, remove the bucket from the machine.
5. Let the loaf cool for 5 minutes.
6. Gently shake the bucket to remove the loaf, and turn it out onto a rack to cool.

Greek Blueberry Bread

Makes 1½ to 2 pounds

- 1 cup plain Greek yogurt, at room temperature
- ½ cup milk, at room temperature
- 3 tablespoons butter, at room temperature
- 2 eggs, at room temperature
- ½ cup sugar
- ¼ cup light brown sugar
- 1 teaspoon pure vanilla extract
- ½ teaspoon lemon zest
- 2 cups all-purpose flour
- 1 tablespoon baking powder
- ¾ teaspoon salt
- ¼ teaspoon ground nutmeg
- 1 cup blueberries

1. Place the yogurt, milk, butter, eggs, sugar, brown sugar, vanilla, and zest in your bread machine.
2. Program the machine for Quick cycle and press Start.
3. While the wet ingredients are mixing, stir together the flour, baking powder, salt, and nutmeg in a medium bowl.
4. After the first fast mixing is done and the machine signals, add the dry ingredients.
5. When the second Mixing cycle is complete, stir in the blueberries.
6. When the loaf is done, remove the bucket from the machine.
7. Let the loaf cool for 5 minutes.
8. Gently shake the bucket to remove the loaf, and turn it out onto a rack to cool.

Pumpkin Bread

Makes 1½ to 2 pounds

- Butter for greasing the bucket
- 1½ cups pumpkin purée
- 3 eggs, at room temperature
- 1/3 cup melted butter, cooled
- 1 cup sugar
- 3 cups all-purpose flour
- 1½ teaspoons baking powder
- ¾ teaspoon ground cinnamon
- ½ teaspoon baking soda
- ¼ teaspoon ground nutmeg
- ¼ teaspoon ground ginger
- ¼ teaspoon salt
- Pinch ground cloves

1. Lightly grease the bread bucket with butter.
2. Add the pumpkin, eggs, butter, and sugar.
3. Program the machine for Quick cycle and press Start.
4. Let the wet ingredients be mixed by the paddles until the first fast Mixing cycle is finished, about 10 minutes into the cycle.
5. While the wet ingredients are mixing, stir together the flour, baking powder, cinnamon, baking soda, nutmeg, ginger, salt, and cloves until well blended.
6. Add the dry ingredients to the bucket when the second fast Mixing cycle starts.
7. Scrape down the sides of the bucket once after the dry ingredients are mixed into the wet.
8. When the loaf is done, remove the bucket from the machine.
9. Let the loaf cool for 5 minutes.
10. Gently shake the bucket to remove the loaf, and turn it out onto a rack to cool.

Nut and Seed Breads

Chapter

6

Caraway Rye Bread

Makes 1 pound

- ¾ cup lukewarm water
- 1 tablespoon unsalted butter, diced
- 1 tablespoon molasses
- ½ cup rye flour
- 1 cup plain bread flour
- ½ cup whole wheat flour

- 1 tablespoon milk powder
- ¾ teaspoon salt
- 2 tablespoons brown sugar
- 1 tablespoon caraway seeds
- 1¼ teaspoons instant dry yeast

1. Add the ingredients into the bread machine as per the order of the ingredients listed above or follow your bread machine's instruction manual.
2. Select the Whole Wheat cycle and medium crust function.
3. When ready, turn the bread out onto a drying rack and allow it to cool, then serve.

Flax and Sunflower Seed Bread

Makes 1 pound

- ²⁄₃ cup lukewarm water
- 1 tablespoon butter, softened
- 1½ tablespoons honey
- ¾ cup bread flour
- ²⁄₃ cup whole wheat flour

- ½ teaspoon salt
- ½ teaspoon active dry yeast
- ¼ cup flax seeds
- ¼ cup sunflower seeds

1. Place all ingredients (except the sunflower seeds) into the bread machine, either in the order listed, or according to your bread machine's instruction manual.
2. Select the Basic cycle, as well as the soft or medium crust function.
3. Just before your bread machine enters its final Kneading cycle (most machines will signal you with a beep around this time), add the sunflower seeds.
4. When ready, turn the bread out onto a drying rack so it can cool, then serve.

Pecan and Walnut Bread

Makes 1 pound

- ²/₃ cup lukewarm water
- 1¹/₃ tablespoons olive oil
- 1¹/₃ tablespoons honey
- 1¹/₃ tablespoons molasses
- 1 teaspoon salt

- ²/₃ cup whole wheat flour
- 1¹/₃ cups plain bread flour
- 1½ teaspoons active dry yeast
- ¼ cup pecan nuts
- ¼ cup walnuts

1. Place all ingredients (except the pecans and walnuts) into your bread machine, either in the order listed, or according to the instruction manual that came with your bread machine.
2. Select the Basic cycle setting and choose the soft crust function.
3. Before the final Kneading cycle, add your pecans and walnuts.
4. When ready, turn the bread out onto a drying rack so it can cool, then serve.

Pecan Rye Bread with Raisins

Makes 2 pounds

- 1¼ cups pecan halves
- 1½ cups water
- 1½ tablespoons butter, cut into pieces
- 3¹/₃ cups bread flour
- ²/₃ cup dark rye flour
- 1½ tablespoons dark brown sugar

- 1 tablespoon plus 2 teaspoons gluten
- 2 teaspoons salt
- 2½ teaspoons SAF yeast or 1 tablespoon bread machine yeast
- ½ cup dark raisins

1. Preheat the oven to 350ºF (180ºC).
2. Spread the nuts on a baking sheet. Bake for 10 minutes, stirring twice. Cool on the baking sheet. Chop the nuts into large pieces and set aside.
3. Place the ingredients, except the nuts and the raisins, in the pan according to the order in the manufacturer's instructions. Set crust on medium and program for the Basic or Fruit and Nut cycle; press Start. When the machine beeps, or between Knead 1 and Knead 2, add the nuts and the raisins.
4. When the baking cycle ends, immediately remove the bread from the pan and place it on a rack. Let cool to room temperature before slicing.

Multigrain Cereal Loaf

Makes 1 pound

- ½ cup milk, warmed
- 2 tablespoons unsalted butter
- 1½ cups plain bread flour
- ½ cup multigrain cereal

- ¼ cup granulated brown sugar
- ¾ teaspoon salt
- ¾ teaspoon bread machine yeast

1. Add the ingredients into the bread machine as per the order of the ingredients listed above or follow your bread machine's instruction manual.
2. Select the Basic cycle and medium crust function.
3. When ready, turn the bread out onto a drying rack and allow it to cool, then serve.

Potato Caraway Seed Bread

Makes 2 pounds

- 1²/₃ cups warm water
- 3 tablespoons instant potato flakes
- 2 tablespoons butter or lard
- 3½ cups bread flour
- ½ cup potato starch flour
- 2 tablespoons sugar

- 1 tablespoon gluten
- 1 tablespoon caraway seeds
- 2 teaspoons salt
- 2 teaspoons SAF yeast or 2½ teaspoons bread machine yeast

1. Place the instant potato flakes in the water in a bowl. Let stand for 5 minutes. The flakes will expand and soften, and the water become cloudy.
2. Place the ingredients in the pan according to the order in the manufacturer's instructions, adding the potato water with the butter or lard as the liquid ingredients. Set crust on dark and program for the Quick Yeast Bread or Rapid cycle; press Start. The dough ball will be smooth and soft. If the dough rises more than two-thirds of the way up the pan, gently deflate the dough a bit. This will keep the dough from hitting the window during baking.
3. When the baking cycle ends, immediately remove the bread from the pan and place it on a rack. Let cool to room temperature before slicing.

Mixed Seed Loaf

Makes 1 pound

- ²/₃ cup lukewarm water
- ²/₃ teaspoon salt
- 1 tablespoon and 1 teaspoon olive oil
- ²/₃ cup whole wheat flour
- 1¹/₃ cups white bread flour
- 1 teaspoon active dry yeast
- 2 teaspoons linseed
- 2 teaspoons pumpkin seeds
- 2 teaspoons sesame seeds
- 2 teaspoons poppy seeds
- 2 teaspoons sunflower seeds

1. Add all ingredients to your bread machine in the exact order listed. Seeds can be added in any order, as long as they come after the yeast.
2. Select the Basic cycle, along with any crust function you desire.
3. When ready, turn the bread out onto a drying rack so it can cool, then serve.

Date and Almond Bread

Makes 1 pound

- ²/₃ cup lukewarm water
- 1 tablespoon vegetable oil
- 1¹/₃ tablespoons honey
- ¼ teaspoon salt
- ½ cup rolled oats
- ½ cup whole wheat flour
- ½ cup bread flour
- 1 teaspoon active dry yeast
- ¹/₃ cup dates, chopped and pitted
- ¹/₃ cup almonds, chopped

1. Add all ingredients (except the dates and almonds) to the bread machine, either in the order listed, or according to your bread machine's instruction manual.
2. Select the nut and raisin setting, as well as the soft crust function.
3. Just before your bread machine enters its final Kneading cycle (most machines will signal you with a beep around this time), add the dates and almonds.
4. When ready, turn the bread out onto a drying rack so it can cool, then serve.

Poppy Seed Almond Bread with Currants

Makes 1½ pounds

- 1 cup plus 2 tablespoons fat-free milk
- 1 egg yolk
- 1 teaspoon almond extract
- 1 (1-pound / 454-g) box white bread machine mix
- ½ cup chopped slivered blanched almonds
- ⅓ cup currants
- 1 tablespoon poppy seeds
- 1 tablespoon light brown sugar
- 2 teaspoons gluten
- 1 yeast packet (included in mix)

1. Place all the ingredients in the pan according to the order in the manufacturer's instructions. Set the crust for medium and program for the Basic cycle; press Start.
2. When the baking cycle ends, immediately remove the bread from the pan and place it on a rack. Let cool to room temperature before slicing.

Walnut and Fig Bread

Makes 1½ pounds

- 1 cup plus 2 tablespoons water
- 1 (1-pound / 454-g) box white bread machine mix
- 2 teaspoons gluten
- 1 yeast packet (included in mix)
- ¾ cup chopped dried figs
- ¼ cup chopped walnuts

1. Place the ingredients, except the figs and walnuts, in the pan according to the order in the manufacturer's instructions. Set the crust for dark and program for the Basic or Fruit and Nut cycle; press Start. When the machine beeps, or between Knead 1 and Knead 2, add the figs and walnuts.
2. When the baking cycle ends, immediately remove the bread from the pan and place it on a rack. Let cool to room temperature before slicing.

Whole Wheat Pine Nut Bread

Makes 2 pounds

- $^2/_3$ cup water
- $^2/_3$ cup dry white wine
- $^1/_3$ cup olive oil
- $2^2/_3$ cups bread flour
- 1 cup whole wheat flour
- $^1/_3$ cup rye flour
- 1 tablespoon plus 1 teaspoon gluten
- 1 tablespoon plus 2 teaspoons sugar
- 2 teaspoons salt
- $2^1/_2$ teaspoons SAF yeast or 1 tablespoon bread machine yeast
- $^1/_2$ cup pine nuts, coarsely chopped

1. Place the ingredients, except the pine nuts, in the pan according to the order in the manufacturer's instructions. Set crust on medium and program for the Basic or French cycle; press Start. Five minutes into Knead 2, sprinkle in the pine nuts.
2. When the baking cycle ends, immediately remove the bread from the pan and place it on a rack. Let cool to room temperature before slicing.

Buttermilk Sunflower Seed Bread

Makes 2 pounds

- $1^1/_3$ cups buttermilk
- 1 large egg
- 3 tablespoons sunflower seed oil
- $2^1/_2$ cups bread flour
- 1 cup whole wheat flour
- $^1/_2$ cup cornmeal
- $^2/_3$ cup raw sunflower seeds
- 3 tablespoons dark brown sugar
- 2 tablespoons gluten
- 2 teaspoons salt
- $2^1/_2$ teaspoons SAF yeast or 1 tablespoon bread machine yeast

1. Place all the ingredients in the pan according to the order in the manufacturer's instructions. Set crust on dark and program for the Whole Wheat cycle; press Start.
2. When the baking cycle ends, immediately remove the bread from the pan and place it on a rack. Let cool to room temperature before slicing.

Orange Cumin Seed Bread

- ²/₃ cup orange juice
- 1 cup fat-free milk
- 4 tablespoons butter, cut into pieces
- 3½ cups bread flour
- ½ cup whole wheat flour
- ¹/₃ cup light brown sugar
- 1 tablespoon plus 1 teaspoon gluten
- 2 teaspoons cumin seed, crushed in a mortar and pestle
- 2 teaspoons salt
- 2¼ teaspoons SAF yeast or 2¾ teaspoons bread machine yeast

1. Place all the ingredients in the pan according to the order in the manufacturer's instructions. Set crust on dark and program for the Basic cycle; press Start. The dough ball will be firm and smooth, yet springy.
2. When the baking cycle ends, immediately remove the bread from the pan and place it on a rack. Let cool to room temperature before slicing.

Oatmeal Walnut Bread

- ²/₃ cup lukewarm water
- ½ tablespoon vegetable oil
- ½ teaspoon lemon juice
- 1 teaspoon salt
- ⅙ cup molasses
- ¹/₃ cup quick oatmeal
- ½ cup whole wheat flour
- 1¹/₃ cup plain bread flour
- 1½ cups walnuts
- 1½ teaspoons instant dry yeast

1. Add the ingredients into the bread machine as per the order of the ingredients listed above or follow your bread machine's instruction manual.
2. Select the Basic cycle and soft crust function.
3. When ready, turn the bread out onto a drying rack and allow it to cool, then serve.

Sesame Seed and Aniseed Bread

Makes 2 pounds

- 1½ cups water
- 3⅓ cups bread flour
- ⅔ cup whole wheat flour
- 1 tablespoon sesame seeds
- 1 tablespoon aniseeds

- 2½ teaspoons salt
- 2½ teaspoons SAF yeast or 1 tablespoon bread machine yeast
- 2 tablespoons yellow cornmeal, for sprinkling

1. Place all the dough ingredients in the pan according to the order in the manufacturer's instructions. Program for the Dough cycle; press Start.
2. Turn the dough out onto a work surface and divide it into 2 equal portions. Knead each portion into a ball and let rest for 10 minutes covered with a clean tea towel. With your fingers, moisten the surface of each dough ball with some olive oil; press with your palm to flatten each into a disc 1 inch thick and 6 inches in diameter. Dust the work surface with a bit of flour to keep the dough from sticking to it and cover the discs with the towel. Let rest for 1½ to 2 hours, until puffy. Prick the surface of each loaf with the tines of a fork to gently release the gas.
3. Preheat the oven to 400ºF (205ºC). Sprinkle a baking sheet with cornmeal and place the loaves on the baking sheet.
4. Immediately place the loaves in the oven (it won't be up to temperature or hot yet) and bake for exactly 12 minutes. Reduce the oven temperature to 300ºF (150ºC) and bake for an additional 35 to 40 minutes, or until the breads are brown and sound hollow when tapped on the bottom with your finger. Remove to a rack to cool before cutting into wedges to serve.

Specialty Flour Breads

Chapter
7

Honey Cornmeal Bread

Makes 2 pounds

- 1½ cups water
- 2 tablespoons unsalted butter cut into pieces
- ¼ cup honey
- 3½ cups bread flour
- ½ cup yellow cornmeal
- ½ cup dry buttermilk powder
- 1 tablespoon plus 2 teaspoons gluten
- 1½ teaspoons salt
- 2½ teaspoons SAF yeast or 1 tablespoon bread machine yeast

1. Place all the ingredients in the pan according to the order in the manufacturer's instructions. Set crust on dark and program for the Basic cycle; press Start.
2. When the baking cycle ends, immediately remove the bread from the pan and place it on a rack. Let cool to room temperature before slicing.

Hominy Cornmeal Bread

Makes 2 pounds

- ²/₃ cup milk
- ²/₃ cup water
- 3 tablespoons olive oil
- 4 cups bread flour
- ²/₃ cup yellow cornmeal
- 3 tablespoons sugar
- 2 tablespoons gluten
- 2 teaspoons salt
- 2½ teaspoons SAF yeast or 1 tablespoon bread machine yeast
- 1½ cups canned hominy, rinsed

1. Place all the ingredients, except the hominy, in the pan according to the order in the manufacturer's instructions. Set crust on dark and program for the Basic or Fruit and Nut cycle; press Start. When the machine beeps, or between Knead 1 and Knead 2, add the hominy.
2. When the baking cycle ends, immediately remove the bread from the pan and place it on a rack. Let cool to room temperature before slicing.

Polenta, Millet, and Sunflower Seed Bread

Makes 2 pounds

- 1½ cups water
- ¼ cup honey
- 3 tablespoons sunflower seed oil
- 3¼ cups bread flour
- ¾ cup whole wheat flour
- $1/_3$ cup polenta
- ¼ cup whole raw millet
- ¼ cup raw sunflower seeds
- 2 tablespoons gluten
- 2 teaspoons salt
- 2½ teaspoons SAF yeast or 1 tablespoon bread machine yeast

1. Place all the ingredients in the pan according to the order in the manufacturer's instructions. Set crust on medium and program for the Basic or Whole Wheat cycle; press Start.
2. When the baking cycle ends, immediately remove the bread from the pan and place it on a rack. Let cool to room temperature before slicing.

Buckwheat Orange Bread

Makes 2 pounds

- $1^1/_3$ cups buttermilk
- 1 large egg
- 3 tablespoons unsalted butter, cut into pieces
- 3 cups bread flour
- 1 cup whole wheat flour
- ½ cup light buckwheat flour
- 3 tablespoons dark brown sugar
- Grated zest of 1 large orange
- 1 tablespoon plus 1 teaspoon gluten
- 2 teaspoons salt
- 2½ teaspoons SAF yeast or 1 tablespoon bread machine yeast

1. Place all the ingredients in the pan according to the order in the manufacturer's instructions. Set crust on dark and program for the Basic cycle; press Start. The dough ball will be moist and springy.
2. When the baking cycle ends, immediately remove the bread from the pan and place it on a rack. Let cool to room temperature before slicing.

Millet Buckwheat Bread

Makes 2 pounds

- 1½ cups water
- 2 tablespoons unsalted butter, cut into pieces
- 3 tablespoons dark honey
- 3½ cups bread flour
- ½ cup light buckwheat flour
- ½ cup whole millet
- 1 tablespoon plus 1 teaspoon gluten
- 2 teaspoons salt
- 2½ teaspoons SAF yeast or 1 tablespoon bread machine yeast

1. Place all the ingredients in the pan according to the order in the manufacturer's instructions. Set crust on dark and program for the Basic cycle; press Start.
2. When the baking cycle ends, immediately remove the bread from the pan and place it on a rack. Let cool to room temperature before slicing.

Pecan Chestnut Bread

Makes 2 pounds

- 1⅛ cups fat-free milk
- 1 large egg
- 4 tablespoons butter or margarine, cut into pieces
- 3¼ cups bread flour
- ¾ cup chestnut flour
- 3 tablespoons dark brown sugar
- 3 tablespoons minced pecans
- 1 tablespoon plus 1 teaspoon gluten
- 2 teaspoons salt
- 2½ teaspoons SAF yeast or 1 tablespoon bread machine yeast

1. Place all the ingredients in the pan according to the order in the manufacturer's instructions. Set crust on medium or dark and program for the Basic cycle; press Start. The dough ball will be moist and springy.
2. When the baking cycle ends, immediately remove the bread from the pan and place it on a rack. Let cool to room temperature before slicing.

Chestnut Polenta Bread

Makes 2 pounds

- 1⅓ cups buttermilk
- ¼ cup dark honey
- ¼ cup olive oil
- 3 cups bread flour
- ¾ cup chestnut flour
- ½ cup polenta

- 2 tablespoons gluten
- 2 teaspoons salt
- 2¾ teaspoons SAF yeast or 1 tablespoon plus ¼ teaspoon bread machine yeast

1. Place all the ingredients in the pan according to the order in the manufacturer's instructions. Set crust on dark and program for the Basic cycle; press Start. The dough ball will be firm, yet slightly sticky.
2. 2 When the baking cycle ends, immediately remove the bread from the pan and place it on a rack. Let cool to room temperature before slicing.

Cinnamon Whole Wheat Barley Bread

Makes 2 pounds

- 1½ cups water
- 3 tablespoons light brown sugar
- 3 tablespoons vegetable oil
- 3 cups bread flour
- ⅔ cup barley flour
- ⅓ cup whole wheat flour

- ¼ cup dry buttermilk powder
- 2 tablespoons gluten
- 1½ teaspoons ground cinnamon
- 2 teaspoons salt
- 2½ teaspoons SAF yeast or 1 tablespoon bread machine yeast

1. Place all the ingredients in the pan according to the order in the manufacturer's instructions. Set crust on medium and program for the Basic or Whole Wheat cycle; press Start.
2. When the baking cycle ends, immediately remove the bread from the pan and place it on a rack. Let cool to room temperature before slicing.

Honey Soy Bread

- 1½ cups water
- 3 tablespoons canola oil
- 3 tablespoons honey
- 3 tablespoons dark brown sugar
- 1 large egg
- 2 cups whole wheat flour
- 1½ cups bread flour
- ½ cup full-fat soy flour
- 2 tablespoons wheat germ
- ⅓ cup nonfat dry milk
- 2 tablespoons gluten
- 2 teaspoons salt
- 1 tablespoon SAF yeast or 1 tablespoon plus ½ teaspoon bread machine yeast

1. Place the ingredients in the pan according to the order in the manufacturer's instructions. Set crust on dark and program for the Whole Wheat cycle; press Start.
2. When the baking cycle ends, immediately remove the bread from the pan and place it on a rack. Let cool to room temperature before slicing.

Honey Teff Bread

- 1½ cups water
- 3 tablespoons vegetable oil
- 3 tablespoons honey
- 3¼ cups bread flour
- ¾ cup ivory or dark teff flour
- 1 tablespoon plus 2 teaspoons gluten
- 2 teaspoons salt
- 1 tablespoon SAF yeast or 1 tablespoon plus ½ teaspoon bread machine yeast

1. Place all the ingredients in the pan according to the order in the manufacturer's instructions. Set crust on dark and program for the Basic cycle; press Start.
2. When the baking cycle ends, immediately remove the bread from the pan and place it on a rack. Let cool to room temperature before slicing.

Jams, PreServes, and Chutneys

Strawberry Jam

Makes 2½ cups

- 1 pound (454 g) fresh strawberries, rinsed, drained, and hulled
- 1 tablespoon fresh lemon juice
- ¾ (2-ounce / 57-g) box powdered fruit pectin
- 1 cup sugar, or to taste

1. Coarsely crush the berries with a potato masher, or put them in a food processor and pulse a few times, leaving a few whole berries or chunks. You will have about 2½ cups. Place the fruit in the bread pan. Add the lemon juice and sprinkle with the pectin. Let stand for 10 minutes. Add the sugar.
2. Program the machine for the Jam cycle and press Start. When the machine beeps at the end of the cycle, carefully remove the pan with heavy oven mitts. You can scrape the jam into heat-resistant jars right away, using a rubber spatula. For other jars, let the jam sit in the pan for 15 minutes before transferring. Let stand until cool. Cover and store in the refrigerator for up to 2 months, or spoon into small freezer bags and freeze.

Apple Pumpkin Butter

Makes 3 cups

- 1 (15-ounce / 425-g) can pumpkin purée
- ¾ cup peeled, cored, and coarsely grated fresh Pippin, Granny Smith, or other firm, tart cooking apple
- ½ cup unsweetened, unfiltered apple juice
- ½ cup light brown sugar
- ½ teaspoon ground cinnamon
- ½ teaspoon ground nutmeg
- ½ teaspoon ground cloves
- 3 tablespoons unsalted butter

1. Combine all the ingredients in the bread pan.
2. Program the machine for the Jam cycle and press Start. When the machine beeps at the end of the cycle, carefully remove the pan with heavy oven mitts. Stir in the butter until it melts. You can scrape the fruit butter into heat-resistant jars right away, using a rubber spatula. For other jars, let the fruit butter sit in the pan for 15 minutes before transferring. Let stand until cool. Store, covered, in the refrigerator for up to 2 months, or spoon into small freezer bags and freeze.

Easy Boysenberry Jam

Makes 2 cups

- 2½ cups fresh boysenberries, rinsed
- 1 (2-ounce / 57-g) box powdered

- fruit pectin
- 1 cup sugar, or to taste
- 2 tablespoons fresh lemon juice

1. Combine all the ingredients in the bread pan. Let stand for 15 minutes to dissolve the sugar.
2. Program the machine for the Jam cycle and press Start. When the machine beeps at the end of the cycle, carefully remove the pan with heavy oven mitts. You can scrape the jam into heat-resistant jars right away, using a rubber spatula. For other jars, let the jam sit in the pan for 15 minutes before transferring. Let stand until cool. Store, covered, in the refrigerator for up to 2 months, or spoon into small freezer bags and freeze.

Mango and Raisin Chutney

Makes 2 cups

- 2 fresh firm-ripe mangoes (about 1½ pounds / 680 g)
- ¼ cup dark or golden raisins, chopped
- 1 medium shallot, minced
- ½ cup dark brown sugar
- A scant tablespoon of minced fresh

- ginger
- 2 teaspoons hot pepper flakes
- Pinch of ground cloves
- ⅛ teaspoon salt
- ½ cup apple cider vinegar
- 2 tablespoons fresh lime juice

1. Peel the mango by standing the fruit stem (wider) end up. Make 4 vertical slices, through the skin, to score the thin tough skin and divide the fruit into quarters lengthwise. Starting at the top, peel the skin back from each quarter, just like a banana. Slice the flesh away from the flat seed in strips. Coarsely chop. You will have about 2 cups.
2. Combine all the ingredients in the bread pan.
3. Program the machine for the Jam cycle and press start. When the machine beeps at the end of the cycle, carefully remove the pan with heavy oven mitts. You can scrape the chutney into heat-resistant jars right away, using a rubber spatula. For other jars, let the chutney sit in the pan for 15 minutes before transferring. Let stand until cool. Store, covered, in the refrigerator for up to 2 months. Serve at room temperature.

Fresh Blueberry Jam

Makes 2 cups

- 1 pound (454 g) fresh blueberries, rinsed
- ½ (2-ounce / 57-g) box powdered fruit pectin
- 1½ cups sugar, or to taste
- 3 tablespoons crème de cassis liqueur
- 2 tablespoons fresh lemon juice

1. Combine all the ingredients in the bread pan. Let stand for 15 minutes to dissolve the sugar.
2. Program the machine for the Jam cycle and press Start. When the machine beeps at the end of the cycle, carefully remove the pan with heavy oven mitts. You can scrape the jam into heat-resistant jars right away, using a rubber spatula. For other jars, let the jam sit in the pan for 15 minutes before transferring. Let stand until cool. Store, covered, in the refrigerator for up to 2 months, or spoon into small freezer bags and freeze.

Cinnamon Apple Butter

Makes 2 cups

- ¼ pound (113 g) dried apple rings, chopped
- 1¼ cups unsweetened, unfiltered apple juice
- 2 tablespoons apple cider vinegar
- 1½ teaspoons ground cinnamon
- ½ teaspoon ground allspice
- ½ teaspoon ground cloves

1. Combine all the ingredients in the bread pan. Let stand at room temperature for 1 hour to soften the apples.
2. Program the machine for the Jam cycle and press Start. When the machine beeps at the end of the cycle, carefully remove the pan with heavy oven mitts and let cool until warm.
3. Using a rubber spatula, scrape the mixture into a food processor fitted with the metal blade and process until smooth. Scrape the apple butter into a glass jar. Let stand at room temperature until cool. Store, covered, in the refrigerator for up to 2 months.

Bing Cherry Jam

- 1 pound (454 g) pitted fresh Bing cherries (you will have both whole cherries and pieces after the pitting)
- 1 cup sugar, or to taste
- 1 tablespoon fresh lemon juice
- Pinch of salt
- 1½ tablespoons powdered fruit pectin

1. Combine the cherries, sugar, lemon juice, and salt in the bread pan. Let stand for 15 minutes to dissolve the sugar. Sprinkle with the pectin.
2. Program the machine for the Jam cycle and press Start. When the machine beeps at the end of the cycle, carefully remove the pan with heavy oven mitts. You can scrape the jam into heat-resistant jars right away, using a rubber spatula. For other jars, let the jam sit in the pan for 15 minutes before transferring. Let stand until cool. Store, covered, in the refrigerator for up to 2 months, or spoon into small freezer bags and freeze.

Peach Jam

- 3 to 4 large peaches (about 1 pound / 454 g)
- 1 cup sugar, or to taste
- 2 tablespoons fresh lemon juice
- 1 (2-ounce / 57-g) box powdered fruit pectin

1. Peel and pit the peaches. Coarsely crush by hand with a potato masher, or pulse a few times in the food processor. You will have about 2½ cups.
2. Combine the peaches, sugar, and lemon juice in the bread pan. Let stand for 30 minutes to dissolve the sugar. Sprinkle with the pectin.
3. Program the machine for the Jam cycle and press Start. When the machine beeps at the end of the cycle, carefully remove the pan with heavy oven mitts. You can scrape the jam into heat-resistant jars right away, using a rubber spatula. For other jars, let the jam sit in the pan for 15 minutes before transferring. Let stand until cool. Store, covered, in the refrigerator for up to 2 months, or spoon into small freezer bags and freeze.

Dried Fruit Apple Chutney

Makes 2 cups

- 2 medium tart cooking apples, peeled, cored, and finely chopped
- ²/₃ cup dark brown sugar
- ¹/₃ cup finely chopped dried apricots
- ¹/₃ cup finely chopped dried pineapple or dried pears
- ¹/₃ cup dark or golden raisins
- ¼ cup finely chopped red bell pepper
- Piece of fresh ginger root about 1 inch long, peeled and grated
- 1 large shallot, finely chopped
- 1 clove garlic, pressed
- ¼ teaspoon ground cayenne pepper
- Pinch of hot pepper flakes
- Pinch of ground turmeric or curry powder
- ½ teaspoon salt
- ²/₃ cup apple cider vinegar

1. Combine all the ingredients in the bread pan.
2. Program the machine for the Jam cycle and press Start. When the machine beeps at the end of the cycle, carefully remove the pan with heavy oven mitts. You can scrape the chutney into heat-resistant jars right away, using a rubber spatula. For other jars, let the chutney sit in the pan for 15 minutes before transferring. Let stand until cool. Store, covered, in the refrigerator, for up to 2 months. Serve at room temperature.

Lemony Raspberry Jam

Makes 3 cups

- 3 cups fresh raspberries, rinsed
- ½ (2-ounce / 57-g) box powdered fruit pectin
- 1¾ cups sugar, or to taste
- 3 tablespoons fresh lemon juice

1. Combine all the ingredients in the bread pan. Let stand for 15 minutes to dissolve the sugar.
2. Program the machine for the Jam cycle and press Start. When the machine beeps at the end of the cycle, carefully remove the pan with heavy oven mitts. You can scrape the jam into heat-resistant jars right away, using a rubber spatula. For other jars, let the jam sit in the pan for 15 minutes before transferring. Let stand until cool. Store, covered, in the refrigerator for up to 2 months, or spoon into small freezer bags and freeze.

Kiwi Jam

Makes 1 ½ cups

- 4 large kiwi (1 pound / 454 g), peeled, sliced, and coarsely chopped
- 2 tablespoons finely julienned lemon zest
- 3 tablespoons fresh lemon juice
- 1 ½ tablespoons powdered fruit pectin
- 1 ½ cups sugar

1. Combine all the ingredients in the bread pan. Let stand for 20 minutes to dissolve the sugar.
2. Program the machine for the Jam cycle and press Start. When the machine beeps at the end of the cycle, carefully remove the pan with heavy oven mitts. You can scrape the jam into heat-resistant jars right away, using a rubber spatula. For other jars, let the jam sit in the pan for 15 minutes before transferring. Let stand until cool. Store, covered, in the refrigerator for up to 2 months, or spoon into small freezer bags and freeze.

Rhubarb and Apricot Jam

Makes 1 ½ cups

- 1 pound (454 g) rhubarb stalks, sliced about ½ inch thick
- 1 ½ cups sugar
- ½ (2-ounce / 57-g) box powdered fruit pectin
- ¼ cup chopped dried apricots

1. Mix the rhubarb with the sugar in a glass bowl, cover loosely with plastic wrap, and let stand at room temperature for 12 hours.
2. Combine the rhubarb-sugar mixture, the pectin, and the apricots in the bread pan.
3. Program the machine for the Jam cycle and press Start. When the machine beeps at the end of the cycle, carefully remove the pan with heavy oven mitts. You can scrape the jam into heat-resistant jars right away, using a rubber spatula. For other jars, let the jam sit in the pan for 15 minutes before transferring. Let stand until cool. Store, covered, in the refrigerator for up to 3 weeks, or spoon into small freezer bags and freeze.

Ketchup

Makes 3 cups

- 1 (28-ounce / 794-g) can tomato purée
- 1 small yellow onion, cut into chunks
- 1 large shallot, chopped
- 1 clove garlic, pressed
- ½ cup apple cider vinegar
- ⅓ cup water
- ¼ cup light brown sugar
- 1 teaspoon ground allspice
- Pinch of ground cinnamon
- Pinch of ground cloves
- Pinch of ground mace
- Pinch of ground ginger
- Pinch of Coleman's dry mustard
- Pinch of crushed hot red pepper flakes
- Fresh-ground black pepper
- Sea salt

1. In a food processor, preferably, or in batches in a blender, combine the tomato purée, onion, shallot, and garlic. Process until just smooth.
2. Pour the tomato mixture into the bread pan. Add the vinegar, water, sugar, and spices.
3. Program the machine for the Jam cycle and press Start. When the machine beeps at the end of the cycle, the ketchup will have reduced slightly and thickened. Add salt and pepper to taste. Carefully remove the pan with heavy oven mitts. You can scrape the ketchup into heat-resistant jars right away, using a rubber spatula. For other jars, let the ketchup sit in the pan for 15 minutes before transferring. Serve warm, room temperature, or chilled. Store covered in the refrigerator for up to 2 months.

Raisin and Ginger Root Peach Chutney

Makes 1¾ cups

- 3 to 4 fresh peaches (about 1 pound / 454 g) or 1 pound (454 g) frozen unsweetened peach slices, defrosted
- Piece of fresh ginger root about 3 inches long
- ⅓ cup golden raisins, chopped
- 2 small white boiling onions, minced
- 1 small clove garlic, minced
- ¾ cup dark brown sugar
- 2 teaspoons chili powder
- 2 teaspoons yellow mustard seeds
- ¼ teaspoon salt
- ½ cup apple cider vinegar

1. Peel the peaches by dipping them briefly into a pan of boiling water to loosen the skins. Immediately cool them by holding them under cold water, and the skins will slip off. Coarsely chop the peaches and place them in the bread pan.
2. Peel and mince the ginger so you have about 2½ tablespoons. You can use a little more or a little less, depending on how hot you want the chutney. Combine the ginger and all the remaining ingredients with the peaches in the bread pan.
3. Program the machine for the Jam cycle and press start. When the machine beeps at the end of the cycle, carefully remove the pan with heavy oven mitts. You can scrape the chutney into heat-resistant jars right away, using a rubber spatula. For other jars, let the chutney sit in the pan for 15 minutes before transferring. Let stand until cool. Store, covered, in the refrigerator for up to 2 months. Serve at room temperature.

Apricot Jam

Makes 2½ cups

- 2 cups pitted and chopped fresh apricots
- 1 tablespoon fresh lemon juice
- ½ (2-ounce / 57-g) box powdered fruit pectin
- 1¼ cups sugar, or to taste

1. Place the apricots and the lemon juice in the bread pan. Sprinkle with the pectin. Let stand for 10 minutes. Add the sugar.
2. Program the machine for the Jam cycle and press Start. When the machine beeps at the end of the cycle, carefully remove the pan with heavy oven mitts. You can scrape the jam into heat-resistant jars right away, using a rubber spatula. For other jars, let the jam sit in the pan for 15 minutes before transferring. Let stand until cool. Store, covered, in the refrigerator for up to 6 weeks, or spoon into small freezer bags and freeze.

Appendix 1 Measurement Conversion Chart

VOLUME EQUIVALENTS(DRY)

US STANDARD	METRIC (APPROXIMATE)
1/8 teaspoon	0.5 mL
1/4 teaspoon	1 mL
1/2 teaspoon	2 mL
3/4 teaspoon	4 mL
1 teaspoon	5 mL
1 tablespoon	15 mL
1/4 cup	59 mL
1/2 cup	118 mL
3/4 cup	177 mL
1 cup	235 mL
2 cups	475 mL
3 cups	700 mL
4 cups	1 L

VOLUME EQUIVALENTS(LIQUID)

US STANDARD	US STANDARD (OUNCES)	METRIC (APPROXIMATE)
2 tablespoons	1 fl.oz.	30 mL
1/4 cup	2 fl.oz.	60 mL
1/2 cup	4 fl.oz.	120 mL
1 cup	8 fl.oz.	240 mL
1 1/2 cup	12 fl.oz.	355 mL
2 cups or 1 pint	16 fl.oz.	475 mL
4 cups or 1 quart	32 fl.oz.	1 L
1 gallon	128 fl.oz.	4 L

TEMPERATURES EQUIVALENTS

FAHRENHEIT(F)	CELSIUS(C) (APPROXIMATE)
225 °F	107 °C
250 °F	120 °C
275 °F	135 °C
300 °F	150 °C
325 °F	160 °C
350 °F	180 °C
375 °F	190 °C
400 °F	205 °C
425 °F	220 °C
450 °F	235 °C
475 °F	245 °C
500 °F	260 °C

WEIGHT EQUIVALENTS

US STANDARD	METRIC (APPROXIMATE)
1 ounce	28 g
2 ounces	57 g
5 ounces	142 g
10 ounces	284 g
15 ounces	425 g
16 ounces (1 pound)	455 g
1.5 pounds	680 g
2 pounds	907 g

CPSIA information can be obtained
at www.ICGtesting.com
Printed in the USA
LVHW062242260622
722166LV00005B/74